I0157196

Last C·O·F·F·E·E with Nonna

Vincent Iezzi

LEONINE PUBLISHERS
PHOENIX, ARIZONA

Copyright © 2014 Vincent Iezzi

Published by Leonine Publishers LLC
P.O. Box 8099
Phoenix, Arizona 85066
USA

All rights reserved. No part of this book may be reproduced or transmitted in any form or by any means, electronic or mechanical, including photocopying, recording, or by any information storage or retrieval system now existing or to be invented, without written permission from the respective copyright holder(s), except for the inclusion of brief quotations in a review.

ISBN-13: 978-0-9860552-9-4

Library of Congress Control Number: 2014947079

Printed in the United States of America
10 9 8 7 6 5 4 3 2 1

Cover design by Tom Pelle, Tamarin Entertainment
www.tamarinent.com

Visit us online at www.leoninepublishers.com
For more information: info@leoninepublishers.com

Dedicated to Nonna's grandchildren

Horace & Joseph Micucci;
Mary Jane, Barbara Ann, and James D'Amore;
Anthony and Diana Marie Iezzi

◆ CONTENTS ◆

◆ PROLOGUE ◆

Nonna always said, "*Quando Dio ci dà qualcosa di ciò che è buono è meglio sempre tenerlo stretto e ricordo che per Dio è buono e, a volte ogni bontà ritorna a lui.*" When God gives us something that is good, it is best always to hold it tightly and cherish it, for all goodness returns to Him.

I remember thinking, at the time she spoke these words, that God seems a bit unkind, but as time passed, I learned the wisdom in these words.

God is a giver. He is the Giver of life, of love, joy, and peace; of now and later. With His giving comes His wisdom, for He knows when we need more, or when we have had enough. As soon as I understood what Nonna meant, I realized that Nonna had given me one of those great wisdoms of life. In my lifetime, I have been given many things and many things have been taken. And still, many were laid aside. Though many things have gone, I still remember them and I hold them tightly. I have had moments with my parents, relatives, and friends that cling to me like my own skin and, of course, among these things are Nonna and her stories.

This is my third book about Nonna. In previous books I have relived my days with every typed word. Over and over again at book signings, literary meetings, schools, colleges, societies, and organizations, she was with me. Our moments together have been shared with family and friends—and strangers. I recognized many times over that Nonna was a God-given-gift to me and others. Nonna shared with me what God had given her—being a story teller, and I in turn, have shared her with others. Nonna's stories have helped many people to experience the miracle of family and, above all, what used to be.

Even though our good God called her goodness back to Him many years ago, I know that what I share with others will always remain in their minds and memories. For like all that is good, she is passed down from one age to another. Like so many things of God she is shared and imitated.

I know she waits for me. Hopefully pleased; though she will not allow me to see how pleased she will be. She will most likely slap me on the back of my head and smile, saying, "*Vinzee, si ha una grande bocca.*" Vince, you have a big mouth.

Now it is time to give goodness back and conclude my books of Nonna; to return her completely to God for Him to enjoy the goodness He has created and leave her to everyone's memories.

◆ NONNA'S HOUSE ◆

Often during World War II when the weather was cold or rainy, I would think of my family members in the armed services. Of course, I didn't realize that it didn't rain everywhere at the same time. I never thought that cold or rainy weather in Philly did not mean cold and rainy weather in North Africa, Italy, Normandy, or Germany. I felt so glad that I was young and away from the war. It was at these moments that I felt so secure in Nonna's house. Though there were cold spots in her big house, especially the back bedroom, there were also warm and comfy rooms like the back kitchen, the living room, and the middle bedrooms.

I have so many good memories of bad weather.

I enjoyed watching snow fall and wishing no one would walk on the snow because, undisturbed, it was the most beautiful sight to see. I liked to see the small crystal cover upon the snow. I envied those snowflakes, for they had traveled many, many thousands of feet to come to rest on my street. They could have come from the cloud that Jesus or one of the Saints had walked on. I always imagined God "giving word" that it was winter and it had to snow. All the Saints and Angels would come out of their homes and begin walking, jumping, and even dancing. The snowflakes would loosen and fall down and down and down to earth, to my street, for me to watch.

I loved watching the rain and sitting comfortably dry by the window as the rain bathed the street. The occasional car would speed by and throw off a spray of water. As I gazed at the people running down the street to get home and out of the rain, I would wonder why they were running. They were soaked already so why run. Then there were the people walking with soggy shoes, even though they carried umbrellas. I could never understand why people carried umbrellas; they never seemed to do much good.

When it was lightning, I always smiled because I loved the excitement of lightning. I remember being told not to sit near a window because I might be struck by the lightning. Nonna used to say, "Lightning is God's power and if you get hit by it, you better believe that God wanted you, and only you, with Him."

In the cold winter days when sitting near a window was too chilly, I would take my stance on the couch with a coat thrown over me and a book in my hand. I remember so often the newspapers that were stuffed under the window to keep out the draft and how after a few days they became a weather-beaten brown. They had to be changed quickly so that the window wouldn't let in the outside air.

No matter how many drafts there were in that house; no matter how many leaks we had in the ceiling or how high the snow got, when we were inside and the candle representing our absence was extinguished, it was always warm in Nonna's house.

✦ WE HAD PIZZELLE ✦

One of Nonna's greatest loves was baking. She made homemade cookies and cakes that I have never found duplicated in any bakery or cake store. She had specialties that were phenomenal. The memories of their tastes are momentous, even to this day. She could easily combine flour, water, and sweets, and mix them into an erupted delight.

The one thing that she enjoyed making most was *pizzelle*—Italian waffles. This small, inexpensive delicacy originated in her home region of Abruzzi which is located in central Italy. Nonna gloated over this history with great pride. Every time she made *pizzelle,* she would tell us the story of how those little Italian waffles were created during the Roman Empire. They were enjoyed by the Roman soldiers long before the common people began enjoying them. She would point out that Saint Peter's wife, Saint Perpetua, made *pizzelle* for him, and before Perpetua left Jerusalem for Rome, she made *pizzelle* for Mary, the Mother of Jesus.

The real story was somewhat different. One year, the *Regione di Abruzzi* was being threatened by poisonous snakes, so the people went to a pagan priestess. She told the people that the snakes had to be captured and draped over a statue of a Roman god. This would tame the snakes and then they were to be released into the wild again. Once this was done, the snakes would not bother the people. The people did what she suggested and the snakes became tame for a year. To celebrate this big event, a local baker made a sugar cookie dough and added anise seeds. He baked it between two hot metal plates and created *pizzelle*.

After telling this story Nonna would say, "*E Dio ha benedetto tutte le cucine Italiane.*" And God blessed all Italian kitchens.

Nonna continued the story.

"So many years later when the Italians were saved by Christianity, the people of Abruzzi continued this tradition, only they draped the snakes over a statue of the great *Santa Domenica*—Nonna's Christian name. One year they processed her statue around the towns and the snakes have never come back to bother anyone.

"So, this is why, when I make *pizzelle* I pray to *Santa Domenica* and *La Madonna*, the Blessed Mother, and ask them to thank God for giving the world so great a gift."

In all the years of listening to Nonna telling me stories, this is the only story I can recall that she repeated. Perhaps it was because she wanted to build pride in us for Abruzzi, or to fortify our love of *pizzelle,* or to make us grateful to God for so great a gift. I don't know. All I do know is that Christmas, Easter, or any great occasion is not the same if we don't have *pizzelle*.

◆ THINGS TO BE BETTER ◆

Nothing entering Nonna's back kitchen was wasted. She had an art for using every morsel of meat, vegetable, bread, and every ounce of liquid. Leftovers were meticulously re-created and disguised into a new, delicious meal. Never a question was asked, for everyone knew that whatever they were eating was carefully prepared.

Hard and old bread was grated and made into crumbs to bread veal, pork chops, and chicken, or as a key ingredient to making meatballs. Fat from meat was turned into lard. Chicken parts were disguised and made into omelets or used for homemade chicken soup.

"God never wasted anything. When He created the world, He wasted nothing, so following His example we must do the same," Nonna said when I questioned her about not wasting anything.

Then one day she broke the mold. After cleaning fish for our meatless Friday, she stood looking down at the fish heads on the table. They were lying there with their eyes open and mouths gaping wide, resting on an old soaked newspaper. After waiting several moments, she turned and went to the kitchen sink and began vigorously washing her hands. She returned to the table and with a *mapeen* dish towel in her hand she wiped her hands dry.

"Vinzee," she finally said. "Take these fish heads and put them on the edge of the fence for the cats."

I obeyed quickly knowing that this unusual order had to have a special reason to it. Normally these fish heads were used to make fish stock for soup, but today Nonna had another idea for the fish heads.

After I had done what she instructed and several minutes passed, she told me, "Go back to the fence and see if the cats have eaten the fish heads."

I looked out the window of the back kitchen toward the newspaper sitting on the edge of the fence. The four corners of the newspaper were flapping freely in the wind.

"No, Nonna," I called back.

"Humph! Here." She handed me the salt and pepper shakers. "Go season the fish for the cats."

I immediately ran out into the backyard, climbed on an overturned trash can, and seasoned the fish heads. I climbed down and returned to the kitchen laughing to myself thinking for the first time in my life that Nonna had gone completely insane. As I closed the screened door to the back kitchen door, I saw two alley cats jump the fence and attack the fish heads.

"Nonna, the cats are eating the fish heads!"

"Ah, you see, even the lowest of low have the need for things to be better. Like the poor cats, we have the right from God to want things to be better."

◆ OVER AGAIN ◆

When I was in the first grade at King of Peace School, the children would save their pennies and buy stamps to adopt pagan babies. Each of us was given a book that had many blocks drawn on the pages. We would buy stamps for three cents and apply the stamps to a block on the page of the book. There were 100 blocks on each page. When the page was completed, we would receive a picture of a child in some foreign land and for three dollars we've adopted a pagan baby. After the child was given a name by the student who completed the page, the monies were sent to the foreign missions. Often we were permitted to write to the child and many times we would receive a letter from the child in his or her language. It was all very exciting and important to me and my classmates.

To help accelerate the project, Mother Mary Edward, our principal, announced that the class with the most pagan babies adopted was to be given half a day off from school and no homework for the weekend.

When I told my family of Mother's announcement, I was given all the pennies they didn't need. Soon I led the class with the most pagan babies adopted. In one month's time I had three babies. As the deadline approached, we learned we were not beating the other classes. On the final day, Sister Mary Madeline announced that an anonymous student had purchased five pages of stamps and our class was the winner with the most adopted babies. So we got our half-day off from school and no homework for the weekend.

I arrived home overjoyed with great exuberance and told everyone my class' success. They greeted the news with reservation which deflated my excitement. Nonna was the only one who showed excitement.

"For the good thing that you have done, tomorrow we will have two cups of coffee," she said and this made me happy.

The next day as we sat drinking our first cup of coffee, Nonna asked me if I had decided what names I was going to give the babies. I looked at her with a bit of apprehension. I didn't know if she would be pleased with my choices. In a low voice I said, "I named the first two Philomena and Joseph" (my parent's names). "The other I named Sunday."

The cup remained on Nonna's lips as she looked over the rim. I could tell she was pleased by the gleam in her eyes, and I could see her eyes were moistening. Slowly she lowered the cup and with great grace placed it on the saucer. After a moment, she said: "Sunday… *Domenica* is a nice name. I never had anyone named after me."

Quickly without thought, I blurted out, "She will never be as beautiful as you, Nonna."

With that Nonna quickly rose from her chair and walked to the sink. I heard a small sniffle as she vigorously washed the coffee cup over and over again.

◆ PRAY OFTEN ◆

"Did you ever wish you could do something very important or great, Nonna?"

"We all do something important," Nonna replied with complete certainty as she walked around the kitchen gathering the ingredients she needed to make homemade spaghetti.

"Well, young people don't always feel they are doing anything important or great," I said. "Look at the world. A lot of things are happening. There is a war going on and there are people who need help and I can't do anything to help them."

"Vinzee, you are still young. Your time will come. Never try to get ahead of time because if you do you lose what is given to you in the present. You should learn to enjoy what is in your world. The grown-ups made this world the way it is and God wants them to fix it, so we are at war to fix it. When your time comes, your world may need fixing also and then you will be called on to do something important and great. Until then, enjoy the time of your innocence and do not be in a hurry to grow up."

I didn't know how to answer Nonna. Somewhere in my young mind I knew that she was correct.

"There was a great Italian writer who once said that every living thing had a purpose and that life was finding what that purpose is. Just like raindrops have purpose and the stars and wind and storms have purpose, so you and I have a purpose."

I waited for several quiet moments and finally said, "Nonna, do you think all young people feel like I do?"

"Of course. I know I did when I was young. I wished God would allow me to be a great person. I, even, wanted to do something great and important for the world. I wanted to get a good education and maybe be a great doctor, but that was only a dream; an impossible dream at that. Soon I began to think I should become a great nun."

"A nun?" I shouted in complete shock.

"Yes, a nun, but my father would not have it. My sister Maria had died as a baby and he said he had given God one daughter and could not give another."

I sat looking at her and quickly realized that if her father had not stopped her I wouldn't be where I was. My mother, aunts, and uncle would not be who they were.

I mentally thanked my *bisnonno* for being so selfish.

"So when I saw I could not become a great nun, I decided to become a good cook."

"And Nonna, you are a good cook."

She smiled and without looking at me said, "Really? Then you see I fixed a part of my world."

She laid the plot and I fell into it.

A few moments passed and she looked at me and said softly, "There is always something important young people can do—they can pray and I always believe God listens to the young faster than the old because the young are closer to His creation than the older people are. The old are close to returning to God and have a lot of regrets and sins that need to be forgotten, while the young are closer to having been made by Him and they still have the innocence of birth. So you can do something far greater and far better than I can. You can pray and God will listen to you faster, and if you want to do something greater, pray often."

◆ CROCHET ◆

When I think back to my days of living with Nonna, I recall with ease the back kitchen where she cooked and where most of our talks occurred and her stories came to life. It was a room of life. It was a room that sustained our living; a room that was used by Nonna as a cure-room. I know of many family decisions made in that room. It was her conference room where family fears, problems, misunderstandings, and tears were shared. Nieces, nephews, cousins, in-laws, and friends came to that back kitchen and Nonna became the soother, the teacher, the counselor. As memorable as this room was, there were other rooms in that house which etched deep memories in my mind.

Next to the kitchen, our living room was another place of fond memories. This was the room where the ladies of our home came to rest and be themselves; be Italians. They rested here after a day of hard work in factories and tailor sweat shops; after a day of fears or loneliness; a day of prejudices, silent insults, and harassment. It was also a place of creativity. In this room at night, the silent and personal magic of crocheting took place. In this room the click, click of knitting needles tingled and blended with the voices of unseen personalities from the radio. Crocheting, knitting, and radio all came together to create the magic of life in our house at night. In that room beauty, warmth, and home came to life.

After we ate and the dishes were washed and put away and the kitchen floor was swept and cleaned, Nonna, my mother, Aunt Jenny, and Aunt Millie would retire to the living room.

They would sit in their usual seats. Nonna would sit in one armchair, Aunt Jenny in the other, and my mother and Aunt Millie on the sofa. The radio was turned on and the four of them would settle in for the night. All the lights in the house were turned off except for the one table lamp in the living room. Even today when I'm in a room with one lamp on and I walk into a dark room, it still brings a chill to my being. Then and now my thoughts always rush back to the light from the one lamp in that living room. With all the ladies of the house in their positions, my cousins and I would sit on the floor by the radio and begin a night of listening and imagination. Seldom did anyone talk except to giggle or try to foretell what was to happen next or, and this happened more often, to translate for Nonna.

From these crocheting frenzies I saw doilies, end table scarves, dining room tablecloths, bedspreads, and even window curtains being made. I saw baby hats, baby blankets, booties, and baby dresses being made. When the four of them transferred their energies to knitting, then an array of clothing appeared: dresses, sweaters, scarves, mittens, bonnets, jackets, and blankets for babies and youngsters. For some reason I was always the mannequin. I always was "about the same size as Horace, Joseph, Pauly or Petey." Christmas gifts were made all year long. Wardrobes were filled many months in advance of anticipated births. Wedding gifts were crocheted long before the wedding day. Things were made and put away for some future date and all were welcomed, for the recipient knew the time, love, and care that went into making these gifts. In all, a gift was always ready to be given; there was no need to buy one.

The surprise in all this work—this assembly work—was that they used few designs and their patterns were reproduced more than twice. I saw pine cones, blades of grass, rose buds, blossoming roses, daisies, tassels, trees, and houses designed and imaged on these crocheted masterpieces.

I can still remember how amazed I would get as I watched the needle and their fingers move so quickly. How magical it all was to see plain, straight white thread grow—blossom—into a thing of wonder. I do not know how they were able to do some of the things they did without a plan. It just seemed to come from their fingers into patterns.

One day Nonna asked me to help her wind the store-bought yarn into a ball. This was a very easy job. She would wrap the beginning of the yarn around a piece of paper. Usually the piece of paper was the paper band from around the yarn. I was to hold the yarn around my wrists and Nonna would begin wrapping the yarn around the piece of paper. The strand of yarn would travel from one wrist to the other until it was completely unwound. While we were doing this, I decided to ask her how she knew what design she was going to make when crocheting or knitting.

"It just happens," she said, but she knew that was not a good answer. "You did not like that answer but it is the truth."

I let it go realizing that it was an adult woman's thing and that I was never to know anything more of it. Many years later, when most of the crocheted and knitted things were gone, I wished I had pushed to learn more about the magic of this art.

My generation has lost a lot of respect for the beauty, creativity, and simplicity of our ancestors.

◆ BIGGER, REDDER, AND HOTTER ◆

Across the alley from our house was an old woman who was a great mystery to our entire neighborhood. No one spoke to this woman, not because they didn't like her or didn't want to know her, but because she spoke with a very funny accent and she was extremely difficult to understand. As a result, she was isolated and it seemed as if no one cared about her. One thing I do remember was Nonna always speaking of this woman with a great deal of pity and compassion. For years I heard her refer to that mysterious woman as *la signora strana*—the strange lady. To address people with the article "the" was a common thing in our family, in fact in all Italian families. We had "the milk-ah man"; "the ice-ah man"; "the coal-ah man"; "the bread-ah man"; "the fish-ah man" and many others. But the most famous of them all was "the yellow water man." Yellow water was yellow bleach used to wash clothes. It was sold in gallon bottles by a man who traveled the length of our alley yelling, "Your yellow water man," but for some reason he was known by most as "ya well-ah water man." So it was an excepted thing for this woman to be called "the strange lady." Then suddenly one day Nonna began to refer to the lady as *"La signora dall'altra parte della strada"*—the kind woman across the way. I never questioned her as to why she felt such an understanding of this woman because I thought it was a simple act of kindness on Nonna's part.

One day Nonna was in our back yard working in her "victory garden." A victory garden was the invention of President Roosevelt who asked all Americans to help the cause of the war by growing vegetables, potatoes, and herbs, and of course we complied. In honesty, Italians always had gardens. For years we grew tomatoes, grapes, basil, parsley, rosemary, and peppers. It was expected of us as Italians. After all, most of the Italian immigrants were farmers and the feel of soil on our hands was a natural thing. Of course Nonna was the greatest victory gardener in the world. She was able to make anything grow and everyone knew it.

One day while Nonna tended her "victory garden," I was in the back kitchen doing something unimportant. Suddenly I heard Nonna say "Hello" and then repeat it again. I immediately got the impression she was trying to get someone's attention. I walked to the kitchen door and found Nonna standing on a wooden stool and leaning over our yard fence. Again she said "Hello" and from across the alley came a faint reply that resembled hello. Nonna slowly stepped off the stool with a pleased look on her face. She glanced up and saw me at the door and a wide smile spread across her face.

"Who you talking to, Nonna?" I asked in Italian.

She put her finger to her lips and quickly came to the door and walked into the house.

"I was trying to get friendly with that kind, lonely lady across the alley. You know, the one who talks funny."

I smiled knowing Nonna at times also spoke funny. I was certain the woman did not understand Nonna.

"Do you think she understood you?"

"Not now, but soon," Nonna said with a bit of pride in her tone. "I think I taught her how to say hello."

I smiled and walked away believing that the lady already knew how to say hello.

Two days later, I again heard Nonna speaking to someone. When I went to the door I saw the alley door open and the woman from across the way standing in our yard working the soil of our victory garden with Nonna. For an instant I thought Nonna had finally gotten to the point of understanding this woman. I wondered how she had done such a thing, but soon I discovered they still did not understand each other, but by watching each other work and by doing things in the garden they were communicating. A shake or nod of the head, a touch of the hand, a finger pointing and a finger waving helped them get things understood. When the lady returned to the other side of the alley and into her yard, Nonna locked the alley door. I walked out into the yard.

"Ah, Vinzee," she said with a beaming face, "today I made a new friend. Poor woman was very, very lonely. I invited her to help me with my garden."

"Nonna, you don't need help."

"We all need help. Even the greatest saints and popes needed help. The reason God created so many people is because we are to help each other, so Alveya showed me how to plant peppers."

"Nonna, you know how to plant peppers."

"Not like a Lebanese does," she responded quickly.

"And just what do Lebanese do that is different from what you do?"

"They do it with Lebanese prayers," she replied smiling. "It seems the Lebanese language is older than Italian and so God knows it better."

"Who told you that?"

"Alveya," Nonna stated as she walked into the house with a bit of pride and cockiness in her walk.

I stood in the yard wondering what I had missed and how Nonna had learned so much about the lady across the alley.

From that day on, Nonna and Alveya were friends and from that day on our pepper plants were bigger, redder, and hotter.

◆ FRANCIS ◆

This is another story that I remember Nonna telling me, and again, I do not know why she did. I can only say that she loved Saint Francis and referred to him simply as Lo Santo—the Saint.

The day was warm and bright.

It was a day given by God for all to see that He was a God of love who loved.

Francis walked along the dry dirt road feeling the rays of the sun warm his skin as they seeped through his brown wool robe. His hair was wet from perspiration and he felt the beads of sweat on his face. With appreciation he remembered that several miles ahead in his walk was a small stream that would refresh him. For the tenth or eleventh time he quickly thanked God for His goodness.

Across his face was no smile, yet he was smiling within. It was a usually happy day for him. He was walking with God. All around him was God. Thinking this way made Francis feel as if he were present on the first days of creation, for all around him was the splendor of creation. Nature was the way God created it—it never changed. He was in Eden and around him was God's creation, the second greatest gift of all. The artistic hand of God burst a multitude of colors about him. His ears were filled with the sounds of joy and life. All these things he physically felt were in appreciation of God. All this was pleasing to him. All this was a blessing for he heard God's voice in the sounds of simple life. The Divine painter was singing and giving life before Francis' eyes. All this beauty was for man to enjoy. God had willed that all of creation was to be seen, felt, and appreciated by man. All of nature was God's love letter to humankind. God's breath was in the landscape, constantly giving new shades and tones to the world, and His cleverness was constantly making alterations to the motion of life.

Whenever Francis walked through the countryside, he was constantly filled with an air of freedom and balminess.

Francis continued to walk the dirt road, appreciating more deeply all that was around him, and finally a smile spread across his black-bearded face. Just as quickly the smile dissipated and he grew serious and pensive. He felt something nearby. He felt something important coming to him.

Those who were also walking the road with Francis were suddenly beside him. He greeted them with his silence and they gleefully accepted this. The group continued to walk along in understood silence.

Pacifico said softly, "A blessed day, Father."

"Yes."

"God's goodness is so great on days such as this," remarked Angelo.

"Yes."

Francis started to walk away from them, not to avoid his companions, but out of a need to be alone with the God he knew was with him. Every so often he would feel God's imminent desire to speak to him, to become physically present to him. When this feeling came upon him, he knew something was about to happen that would require him to react. Those around him understood these quick changes in Francis and willingly accepted it.

He continued to walk and soon he was standing in a wide, open field. He stood watching the tall weeds and grass sway and dance freely with the passing fingers of the wind. He was delighted by the uniformity of nature. He was greatly comforted by the sights and sounds around him. Unexpectedly a bird came and sat on his shoulder. Sitting there for a few precious moments, it flew away and began circling Francis. The bird was soon followed by another, and then another, and on it went until Francis was surrounded by birds. Their calls for his attention were deafening, yet beautiful to him. He laughed with sheer and innocent delight at the sight about him. He twirled around enjoying the rainbow of colors that the different birds created. When on the verge of falling to the dirt, he stopped and slowly the birds began to settle before him like students before a teacher.

"Ah, my brothers, you are seeking some knowledge. Shall I speak to you of God? But I am certain you know of Him. You and your ancestors have lived unblemished and free of sin since the beginning of time. Oh, now I know what you want, you want to see if I have learned anything new about our God. Well, I try daily to learn more and more of Him, and I am certain I shall leave this world not knowing all one needs to know of God. I think, all of us get a bit or a piece of Him and that becomes our benchmark."

Francis looked up and saw ravens, hawks, and eagles circling over the field of small birds and for one quick moment he grew fearful for the little birds' safety. Suddenly in an orderly fashion, the bigger birds began to land in the fields, and Francis smiled.

This is the way it should be. He thought. *This is the way all life should be. We should live as one, together, in peace and harmony always in need to know God.*

"Well, my brothers and sisters, I think you have taught me a lesson. I cannot put this lesson into words and I see that you want me to tell you what I have learned. You have such hope in me. Give me time and I will find the right words, with God's help."

He stopped speaking and surveyed all that was before him. Then he picked up two twigs of a tree—one long and one short. He pretended one was a violin and the other a bow, and he began to play a silent rhapsody. All the birds began to sing in perfect harmony and the air and the earth were filled with a beauty never known or experienced before in all time.

With a voice that was as sweet and as pleasant as the sound of the singing birds, Francis put into words the lesson that he was taught by his winged family.

"Lord, make me an instrument of your peace…"

◆ IT WAS DONE ◆

Sister Mary Killian told us during lunch that we were to think of and count the number of miracles we could remember that Jesus had performed. In our afternoon session she would ask us how many we had remembered and the student who was most accurate would get a hundred for a test mark. I was so excited with this assignment that I rushed home for lunch. I knew Nonna *knew* so I would not have to think, count, or look in the Bible. I burst into the house and began running to the back kitchen, shouting, "Nonna, how many miracles did Jesus perform?"

I hurried into the kitchen and found Nonna sitting at the table drinking a cup of coffee and nearby on a dish was my baloney sandwich and cup of coffee.

"What did you want?"

"How many miracles did Jesus perform?"

"I don't know," she replied and immediately my world collapsed and Nonna was an ordinary grandmother.

"Oh Nonna, I thought you would know. Now I have to guess."

I threw myself onto a kitchen chair and lost all desire to eat or drink coffee.

"Why do you need to know?"

"Sister asked us to find out and if we know the right amount we will get a hundred for one of our marks."

"Well then, we will have to think about her question, but first you must calm down and eat and together we will get a good answer for Sister."

She took a sip of her coffee, but I did not calm down.

"*Mo, ci si siede e mangia lentamente.*" Now you sit and eat slowly.

I slowly picked up the sandwich and took a nibble out of it.

Nonna took another sip of her coffee.

"*Mangia.*" Eat, she ordered and I nibbled again.

Moments passed and I watched her and knew she was thinking, so I took a bigger bite and soon saw a smile spread across Nonna's lips.

"How many miracles do you think Jesus performed?"

"About thirty," I answered.

She remained silent.

Moments again passed and after another sip of coffee, she said, "No, I think many, many more. Maybe about a hundred or more."

"Nonna, that is too much."

"Really? I do not think so." She rose from her chair, walked to the kitchen sink, and began washing her cup in suds and water.

After she finished she returned to the table, sat down, and folded her hands as if in prayer.

"Remember Saint John saying in the Bible that not all of what Jesus did or said was in the Bible? Ah, you remember. Good, now think of that when we have to count all His miracles. After you eat I will tell you a story that a great Italian saint wrote many, many years ago."

In three chews my sandwich was finished and the coffee cup was in my hand.

So the story went.

"The road was dry and the dust rose to meet the faces of the travelers. For an instant the clouded air choked their breath and several of the men with Jesus coughed and cleared their throats. But it did not bother Jesus. He walked casually along the road, admiring the sky above and the hills in the near distance. He looked ahead to see two of His younger friends walking side-by-side, occasionally giggling to their whispered conversations. They were young and what was entertaining them was from their innocence, so purity was allowed its moment.

"Behind Him Jesus heard the discussions of His more mature traveling friends. Their voices were raised in debate and some of the voices were far more strained than others. He listened to their conversation and decided not to interfere, for it was important for them to draw conclusions. In spite of His decision to ignore them, Jesus continued to listen and occasionally smiled because of their simplicity and their ignorance.

"Distracting Himself, Jesus looked off the road and into the nearby desolate land. Away in the distance there was a man with a small flock of sheep. Jesus watched as the sheep feverishly searched the barren land for a speck of green grass or shrubs or anything to digest. He was certain even a drop of water would have been a treat for the sheep. Their search was in vain.

"Despite the distance, Jesus could hear the shepherd speaking to his sheep. 'Ah, my poor sheep. You wander in despair for there is nothing to make you satisfied. Forgive me for I am not the Almighty and cannot provide food for you.'

"Jesus felt sympathy for the shepherd, yet returned His attention to His friends who still were debating. Their voices had grown louder and He knew soon they would be coming to Him for some clarification.

"But again Jesus heard the shepherd: 'Come my poor sheep, we shall again go off without any food. Once again you shall long for sustenance and your longing shall cause me to grieve with you.'

"Jesus stopped walking and turned His attention completely to the barren land, the sheep, and the shepherd. He felt the man's soul wrenching with the need to provide for his small flock.

"The two young friends, John and Jude, who had been walking in front of Jesus, walked back to join Him. Their youth was so refreshing to Jesus that He allowed Himself to be distanced from the shepherd and his sheep. As they continued to walk, John and Jude began to mildly ridicule the older men who still were lagging behind them.

"But again, Jesus was distracted by the sound of the shepherd's voice. It was so loud and clear that it would have been easy to think the shepherd was standing beside Jesus.

"'Almighty One, can You grant me, a poor man, a wish? Could You give my sheep some comfort? Can You allow food to feed them so that they may be satisfied? Can You help them be nourished? Show me Your benevolence and let this barren place become a place of plenty.'

"Jesus smiled and John and Jude became overjoyed, for they thought the smile was from their remarks.

"Jesus stopped walking and turned His attention to the barren field. Slowly He raised His eyes to the heavens. The warm sun settled on His face and His mind filled with prayer.

"Out of nowhere came a cooling breeze, and Jesus' lips parted into a broad smile.

"Suddenly the clouds rolled across the sky and rain streamed down from the heavens with great force. Within seconds the barren land was watered and just as suddenly, grass, bushes, and greenery appeared.

"The shepherd fell to his knees in gratitude.

"Those with Jesus raced for protection in a nearby cave, but Jesus continued to walk unbothered by the rain. He entered the cave to join the others, grateful for answered prayer. When He arrived, His robe was dry and Jesus once again had done a great thing with no one knowing it was done."

Nonna stopped and sat back in her chair.

"So you see, Vinzee, Jesus performed many quiet and unnoticed miracles. He had to, for He saw how badly the world needed a Savior and He was too much in love with mankind not to perform such quiet miracles. So like I said, I think Jesus performed many miracles that are not in the Bible." She rose from her chair and began to walk into the living room but stopped. "Just like now, I am certain God is performing a miracle for someone in answer to some prayer and no one knows about it except the person in need."

I picked up my cup and put it in the kitchen sink and began washing it in sudsy water. When I finished, I walked into the living room. Nonna was by the radio listening to one of her Italian stories.

"One thing more, Vinzee. Tell Sister there were so many miracles that they were not all written down. Tell her I said there really was only one miracle that really has to be counted and that was when Jesus became man."

"Thank you, Nonna," I said as I raced back to school.

In class Sister announced that we would go around the room, row by row, student by student, and tell how many miracles Jesus performed. She started with the first row and I was in the sixth row, which was next to the last row.

My classmates began shouting out fifteen, twenty, twenty-five. The most called out was thirty which was my thinking, but when it came to me I shouted, "Over a hundred!" My classmates laughed and smirked and some even gasped.

Sister looked at me and smiled.

When all the class had finished, Sister announced that thirty-seven would be more close to the miracles Jesus performed. A figure no one had.

"Vincent, I am curious as to why you thought there were over one hundred," she asked with a small smile on her face and a gleam of interest.

I stood up and with sweaty hands and a racing heart began telling her and the class Nonna's story. After a few seconds I realized everyone was hanging on my every word. I became calm and even began to elaborate on Nonna's words; a small sin I committed frequently in later years when telling her stories.

Finally I finished the story, and I added Nonna's last remark to me. Sister stood quietly looking at me for several tense moments.

"Where did you read that story?" she asked.

"I didn't read it," I responded. "My Nonna—grandmother—told it to me, Sister."

Again there was silence.

"Your grandmother is a very smart woman."

"I know, Sister."

She smiled.

"I agree with your grandmother, and since no one guessed correctly, I think I will award you the hundred. Do you agree, class?"

The class agreed. Then Sister began to clap in applause and the class followed her example.

When I returned home and told Nonna what had happened, she smiled and said, "Ah you see, Jesus performed another miracle."

"Yes, Nonna, that is right, but you helped."

"No. Jesus just used me to do a small thing for Him, and with no one, not even me, knowing it was done."

◆ WHAT NONNA SAW ◆

During World War II, the civilians made daily sacrifices for their family members in the military and for all of America's servicemen and servicewomen. These sacrifices were done with great understanding but in today's world they would seem by many as being too extreme or too demanding. We were rationed and many of the simplest luxuries of life were hard to get. Gasoline, sugar, coffee, meat, butter, nylon stockings, and tires were some of the things that were hard to buy. Though many were employed and there was some money to spare, we could not buy many things. A lot of the good things in life were not ours to buy, so we enjoyed, understood, and lived with only the simple luxuries of life.

One of these simple luxuries was the radio.

It was free!

It was always there!

In some houses the radio was on all day and that was because radio broadcasts always had a little something for everyone. First off, it was a place of instant news. My heart still beats rapidly when I hear, "We interrupt this broadcast to bring you this latest bulletin..." Those opening words told us of the invasion of Poland, France, the Benelux and Scandinavian countries. They were the opening words to the bombing of Pearl Harbor. On emergency-free news day mornings and afternoons, the radio was filled with the voices of disk jockeys, music, singing, big bands, and soap operas. Most of the time, these shows were heard as Nonna cleaned the house, washed, ironed our clothes, and cooked. She found time for the English soap opera shows such as *Young Doctor Malone, Helen Trent,* and of course *Kate Smith Speaks.* Our favorite was *Our Gal Sunday* only because it gave us an opportunity to tease Nonna. Nonna's name was *Domenica,* which is Italian for Sunday, and every time the show would come on, one of her grandchildren would yell, "Nonna, they are broadcasting your life story." Whenever she could she would tune in to the Italian Radio Stations, with Italian entertainers, songs, and stories. One of the funniest things you might ever hear was the Lone Ranger in Italian. Imagine an American Indian speaking vernacular Italian to a ranger with a Midwest accent and you will get the gist of what I am saying.

Late afternoon, before dinner, the kiddie shows were filled with jungle heroes, magic ladies, secret clubs, and space heroes. When we children came home from school and after doing our homework and household chores, the radio became ours for a few hours and we would listen to *Jack Armstrong, Red Rider,* and of course *Captain Midnight.*

Evening radio was drama, comedy, and mystery. Every night after dinner with the dinner dishes washed and away, our family would settle into the living room. Nonna, my mother, and aunts would sit on the sofa and armchairs crocheting or knitting while we children would sit or lie on the linoleum floor and listen to the radio. The table lamp between the two armchairs would be turned on and usually was the only light on the first floor or in the entire house. The rest of the house was given to and rested in darkness. This one-lighted lamp was like an open fireplace to us. We gathered around it and felt clinging warmth from it, for to be out of the circumference of the light isolated you from the rest of the family. In fact I can literally remember walking away from this light, this family circle, and getting a certain chill, a coldness that stayed with me until I returned to its beam. We sat in silence and in deep concentration, except for a delight-ful giggle or a ventured guess to the solution of a mystery.

I remember Nonna sitting in her favorite armchair by the radio, wearing her frameless eyeglasses and knitting or crocheting. Her legs extended before her and crossed at the ankles. She would listen stoically because a lot of times she did not understand everything being said. She would react when she heard us laugh or react and then in Italian would ask, "What did he say?" "What happened?" and we would quickly translate and then appreciate her true reaction, which usually was an understanding nod or a very simple grin because she did not have our sense of humor.

The radio was a wordless book and the voices we heard were story-tellers and it was so easy to become part of the make-believe. From the radio we listened to movies stars, comedians, and singers. We lived the mysteries, helped the detectives, captured the gangsters, pitied the dumb blondes, and cried with another man's family. Every night of the week we had a special and different visitor to our house.

We had Hollywood greats like Bob Hope, Jack Benny, Eddie Cantor, Kay Kyser, and Burns and Allen visit and stay with us. We laughed with *Henry Aldrich, Luigi, Abbott and Costello,* and *Fibber Magee and Molly.* We shivered and were thrilled by *The Shadow, Inner Sanctum, The Whistler, Suspense, The Fat Man,* and of course *Mister District Attorney.*

Magically they came into our house and became a part of our family for the half hour or hour they were on the air. Even the commercials were part of our lives. We sang their jingles and hummed their tunes and bought their products because the soap floated, or we wanted to know where the yellow went, and we wanted to smoke that cigarette because more doctors smoked it.

Sadly there were radio newsmen and commentators who in the early days of the War gave us much bad news. Men with funny sounding names, yet distinct voices, commented on the world at war. We heard and appreciated voices and men like Edward R. Morrow, Gabriel Heater, Walter Winchell, and K.V. Kaltenborn. Their voices were often serious, grim, almost chilling to the bone and never forgotten; even till this day they echo in our ears and minds. More frightening were the sounds of war: the whistling bombs and sirens. Even the voices of the enemy echoed in our living room.

Perhaps one of the greatest things radio did for us was it made us imagine. If we never saw a picture or did not know what Hope, Cantor, or De Mille looked like, we would create an image. From our ears to our imagination every voice, sound, and action was played out and we created the scene, the face, the place in our minds. Each of us in our own mind's eye created different images, and that was what made radio so great. It gave us the chance to see what we wanted to see the way we wanted to see it. It was ours to make, imagine, and keep. All of radio came to life in us because there was nothing to tell us what we imagined was wrong or that it was incorrect. One thing that did happen was it built misconceptions as in the case of Eddie Cantor and me.

As a child, I was a great fan of Eddie Cantor and loved to hear him speak and sing. I had this image of a short, fat, jovial man with a small young face and a mess of blond hair. Years later when TV came into our lives, I saw Cantor. He had the same voice and sang the same but he was not short, fat, jovial, young, or blond. I never liked him after my first TV sighting of him.

Another amazing thing was how radio got people to talk to each other in stores, on the street, or at work. The day after a radio show aired, people talked about what they heard on radio the night before and how they laughed or cried or were frightened. The radio was one of our greatest escapes during the War and because of it, we lived a great life of family, home, and luxury.

Of all these memories, the one thing I remember most was how Nonna made radio become something more to me. Nonna and I had a daily ritual. When I came home from school she would ask me, "Vinzee, what did you learn new today in school?"

Proudly I would tell her because I wanted to show off and I wanted her to know how smart I was becoming, and because I knew she wanted to learn something new. Many times she would look at me with amazement on her face and say, "Really? Is that the truth?"

One day I came home, and after telling her about the Crusaders and the latest story Sister told us about one of the Saints, I told her the story we had read in Bible History about Joseph being sold by his brothers.

After I had finished I said, "I really don't like that story, Nonna."

"Why? It is a beautiful story."

"Yeah, I guess, but my Bible History book didn't have any pictures in it and I don't know what Joseph looked like."

Nonna ran her hand through my blond hair and said, "Ah, Vinzee, you are young and you have not had the chance to read all the Gospels, so until you do you have to listen. The first thing all great writers do before they begin to write is they listen and once they have done that then they create. You know that everything people create, they create because God wants us to. God wanted us to fly like birds so He made us learn about airplanes. He wanted us to sing so He made us create music. He made us create radio so that we will learn to be still and be quiet, and I think God created radio because He wanted to teach us to listen. That is all God ever asks of us. He is always, from the Garden of Eden to now, telling us to listen to Him. The writers of the Bible, like the writers on the radio, tell us a story. We have to imagine the pictures to the story and the Bible so that we can understand, and see, and listen to what God is saying to us. The radio is a great trainer for us to listen and to see people as we want to see them. God comes out of the pages of the Bible the way we need Him to be, as we want Him to be, as we believe Him to be. So remember, when you imagine God, do not become surprised if His face is the old sick man down the street or the poor lady around the block or the sick and wounded soldier or sailor. If you are blessed you will finally see the face of God the way you need to see it. After you have found what God looks like, He will be alive in you forever."

I did as Nonna said and as always she was right.

Joseph came to look like my father, and Joseph's brothers came to look like my father's brothers and step brothers.

Saint Francis began to look like the thin young man I often saw walking the streets in winter with only a ripped sweater wrapped around him.

Saint Gabriel started to look like Armen, the eighth-grader who Mother Mary Edward sent around with notes and messages for the Sisters.

God the Father became the happy man around the corner who was always whistling and singing and smiling.

God and His Angels and Saints came to me as I needed them to be.

The Blessed Mother came to be the nun who treated me kindly, or the mother who was suffering most because her son was wounded or killed in action.

It always amazed me how Nonna could make God come alive in all things. As time passed, I began to do the same thing in my life, and wondered how others could not see what Nonna saw.

◆ GOD WILL NEVER NEED THAT BRIGHT A STAR ◆

All through my life I have found Nonna's stories helpful to live each day, but there was one time when one of her stories helped me excel with a school assignment. Every year when our summer vacation was over and we students returned to school, we were always asked by our new nun teacher to write what we did during the summer. This was an assignment that went toward our Grammar/English mark, and it was in the form of an essay. This was a much hated and rather hard assignment because most of us just played ball in the streets, in some vacant lot, or in a public park. Few of our families could afford vacations because it was during the War and money was not very plentiful. Not many of us had a convenient means of travel because few of our parents owned or operated automobiles and most of our fathers and male family members were still in the service fighting the War.

When I began fourth grade, my new teacher was Sister Mary Eulalia. She was a very different nun. She never physically punished anyone and that made her quite unique. Her form of punishment was writing. If you misbehaved for talking, you had to write one hundred or five hundred times, "I shall not talk in class." If you were caught running in the school halls, one hundred or five hundred times you would write, "I shall not run in the school halls." Some of us would have preferred a slap on the hand rather than writing because a slap was over in a minute or two, but this punishment lasted a lot longer.

When we returned from vacation that year, Sister asked us to write an essay telling her what we thought heaven was like.

I can remember being disappointed by her assignment and I knew many of my classmates were equally disappointed because they, like me, had taken mental notes all summer long and had their composition mentally outlined for our usual assignment. On hearing this assignment, I immediately realized it was going to demand a lot of thought and imagination.

That very day I began my essay. I sat at the dining room table to write what heaven was like. With a piece of paper in front of me and a pencil in hand (we started using pens and ink in the fifth grade), I waited for God to reveal what heaven was like. All I got was clouds and blue skies, and stars and the moon. I knew I had to write what was beyond that. I wondered what was on the other side of these things. After all, if God's house was there, it had to be more and something very special.

Somebody better help me! I thought.

Soon frustration etched its way onto my face and when Nonna came from the back kitchen and saw me laboring over the blank sheet of paper, she asked, "So what could be so terrible to make you look so sad and confused?"

"I have to write what I think heaven is like."

"Is that all?" she replied and walked back into the back kitchen.

Then suddenly, God was there and He had sent me a messenger. I followed Nonna into the kitchen and found her sifting confectionary sugar over a newly baked cake.

"Nonna, what do you think heaven is like?"

"So, Mister Wise Guy," she said with a wide smile, "you are without an answer? You have so much to say about everything and you cannot think of what heaven is like?"

She gave me a quick glance and her smile widened.

"I think we should have a cup of coffee. Yes?"

I quickly ran to the gas range and threw on the jet, ran to the ice box (we didn't have a refrigerator) for the milk, and on the way back grabbed two cups, two spoons, Karo syrup (sugar was rationed), and two paper napkins.

When all was set, Nonna ordered, "Sit," and I quickly sat and thanked God for my human angel of inspiration.

"Heaven is nothing but clouds."

I froze.

Is that it? Is that all I am going to get? I was about to cry!

"And…"

What a magnificent word! Now I will get the rest of it!

"…all the buildings in heaven are made of clouds. Now these building are nothing like the tall buildings we have in Philadelphia. The buildings in heaven are low and plain and simple, but they are long and sometimes stretch out for many city blocks. I guess you would say they look like long boxes. The most amazing thing about these buildings is they have no doors or windows and some of them do not even have roofs."

She walked to the sink, washed her hands and the sifter for the confectionary sugar in hot sudsy water, and then wiped her hands with the *mapeen* dish cloth. She expertly threw the *mapeen* over her shoulder and strode to a chair and sat. She had completed her daily chores. Dinner was started. Dessert was made. Now she could relax and only put up with me.

"The buildings with no roofs are the buildings where the Messenger Angels and Guardian Angels go to rest, and because they work the hardest, God makes it easy for them to enter their homes. They just fly over the walls of the roofless buildings and into their rooms.

"Now a lot of the angels fly around heaven, but most of them walk and still others travel on clouds. They ride around the blue sky quickly and use the clouds like skis; others fly around slowly with notepads making notes and checking everything. Those that fly around are keepers of stars, the sun and moon, and of the other planets. When they want to enter a building, they simply walk through the fluffy cloudy wall, because as I said, there are no doors or windows to these buildings, and besides they are spirits."

Nonna continued. "As you might have guessed, each building is used for something special. There is the Report Building. This building receives all the reports from the angels of damaged stars, or lack of sunlight, or clouds not being fluffy enough, or the need for rain or snow. This building also receives reports on how the soul of a person is doing on earth. You will find your Guardian Angel's report about you in this building. This is also the building where the book is kept that tells how many good things you did and how many bad things you did. With all the people in the world you can imagine this is a big, big building, and like I said, they are not tall buildings, just wide, long, and very busy buildings."

Nonna went on. "There is the Reception Building which is the building all of us have to enter after we die and before we are judged. When we go to this building, a group of Messenger Angels go around heaven telling everyone who has just arrived. This is the building where all our family, relatives, and friends come to see and greet us. It is also in this building that we are given our new white robes to wear to appear before God for judgment.

"Then there is the Choir Building. Even angels have to practice all their songs of praise to God so there is constant singing in heaven because they are always practicing. In order to be an angel, every angel has to learn all the songs of praise to God. After they have learned all the songs, then they are given a schedule of what times they are to have the special duty to praise and glorify God.

"There is the Repair Building where angel wings are repaired and where clouds are made soft, stars are shined, the moon polished, and the sun cleaned.

"Finally there is the Crying Building. In this building the angels cry…"

Before she continued I interrupted, "Nonna, angels don't cry!"

"Of course they do. How do you think we get rain? But they do not cry because they are sad about anything in heaven; no, they cry because of us. When they see all that we do to hurt God, they become sad and cry, and that becomes rain.

"With all the cabinets, files, desks, and furniture in each of these buildings, sometimes the angels have to move things around and that makes a lot of noise. When they do the moving, we hear the noise down here on earth. Smart people call that noise thunder, but smarter people know the angels are moving cabinets, desks, and furniture."

She sat back in her wooden chair and folded her arms across her breast, and this was my chance to question her.

"Nonna," I asked, "what building does God stay in?"

"He has no house," she answered with a bit of surprise in her voice. "He is God and He is everywhere."

Dopey! You knew that, I thought to myself, and then I quickly gathering my senses. I asked, "Well, what about the saints? Where do they stay and what is their building called?"

"They live in the Honor Buildings. They each have their own office and an angel secretary who helps them sort out all the prayers, petitions, and pleas they receive. The prayers are sorted out by how important or urgent they are. Some are put aside for later days and others are rushed to the saint for his or her immediate attention. Some saints such as Saint Joseph, Saint Francis, Saint Anthony, Saint Rita, and Saint Theresa are busier than others and they sometimes have two or three angel secretaries."

"And where does Mary live?"

"She has a building of her own and has many, many angel secretaries."

She broke her poise and leaned close to the table and gently sipped her coffee.

"And what about the souls of the good people?" I asked.

Nonna smiled.

"They are the ones living on the stars; they are the ones who make the stars bright with their bright souls and they are the ones who wink, blink, and watch over us and pray for us."

The room became quiet.

I had nothing more to ask. Nonna had everything covered.

"How do you know this, Nonna?"

"I dreamed it."

"Dreams are not real," I snapped back feeling very proud, smart, and a bit disappointed, for I thought some wise Italian had written a book about these things or some saint once told a story about heaven.

"Everything in and around life is real. Dreams are part of life and so dreams are real. Look in your Bible and you will see dreams are real. Not everything that is real has to be seen. Spirits are real. Look into your heart and you will find your soul, which is a spirit that you cannot see. Look into your soul and you will find God who always existed as a separate being, a Spirit, who you cannot see. Become quiet and still and you will feel your Guardian Angel, and he is a spirit and also unseen. You might not be able to see everything in life or everything that makes up life but that does not mean they do not exist."

I took a sip of my coffee; it was the quick sip that I used so often to delay Nonna from saying anything more and to give me time to quickly evaluate the new lesson she had taught. It always worked, because without looking at Nonna I knew she was watching me.

I knew Nonna was right again. So, I finished my coffee in three quick full gulps and ran from the room hurrying to get to my blank paper before I forgot anything that was told to me. As I walked away I sensed, I knew, Nonna was smiling to herself, either from self-satisfaction or pleased that she had taught me something new.

I picked up my pencil and began changing the face of the blank piece of paper before me into a masterpiece of scribbled symbols.

The next day I turned in my composition.

Nothing more was said or mentioned about heaven until one week later when I got my essay paper back with 100% written across the top. At the bottom of the page was written, "If heaven is like this, I will try to shine the brightest."

I took the paper home and showed Nonna and she smiled. She took a deep breath; it was her way of showing a bit of pride that seldom and briefly came over her.

With a wide, warm smile on her face and in a strained voice she said, "Tomorrow when you go to class, you tell Sister that she will be the second brightest star, for I will be the brightest because I have a grandson like you."

I walked away from the back kitchen praying that God will never need a star as bright as Nonna.

◆ ONE OF HER STORIES ◆

The two boys sat watching the short, young woman as she walked with great difficulty down the street. The woman was wearing thick eyeglasses and straining to read a note or message in her hands. She held the paper very close to her wrinkled nose as she squinted her eyes. She needed to do this so as to read the words on the paper.

Finally, the two boys looked at each other and began to giggle and they laughed aloud. Having laughed enough, they began to mimic the woman.

Standing nearby were their mother and aunts and when their mother became aware of what the boys were laughing at, they were immediately told to go into the house. As they walked away, she gave them her familiar crooked look that said much more than words spoken.

"Go in the living room and you are to sit still—be quiet—and wait until I come in," their mother said with a great deal of displeasure in her voice.

Quickly the boys' smiles and giggles disappeared as they walked into the house. They knew they were going to be reprimanded when their mother arrived home; yet, they did what they had been ordered to do and went directly into the living room and sat still and silent.

In the distance they heard the voice of the "Righter of Wrongs." They quickly deduced that their mother informed the "Righter of Wrongs" and the boys now realized they were going to be punished. The "Righter of Wrongs" said nothing to them as he walked into the house and into the living room. He sat in the reclining chair opposite them. After a few moments they were asked what they did wrong, and they told of laughing and imitating the woman.

Silence followed and then they were told this story.

"There once was a very big, strong, but dark black bear that roamed the forests of Italy. This bear had the meanest and hungriest look in his eyes. He was so big and so strong that all the animals in the forest feared him because they saw him as the ugliest and the meanest bear in all creation. Whenever he approached the river or the lake to drink, the other animals big and small would scurry away as fast as they could and not look back. The water hole was his for as long as he wanted it, because none of the other animals would dare to disturb him or even go near the lake when he was there. He would drink all he wanted with no interruption from any of the animals in the forest. Even the villagers who lived near the forest were very fearful of this black bear. When the villagers saw him, they would dash away in terror. So with no fear or care, and with little opposition, Big Bear would walk the streets of the village and eat everything and anything he could find, and the villagers would do nothing to stop him. They were so afraid of him that no one even thought to kill him.

"The fear for Big Bear went on for many years until one day something very strange happened in the forest. It was a normal, warm summer day and all the birds were chirping and all the trees were whispering and talking to each other as the breeze passed through their leaves. The shrubs were dancing and swaying in the soft breeze and all the animals were playing happily.

"Suddenly, Mother Squirrel let out a loud scream. Her baby squirrel had fallen from the tree and landed on the soft green grass below and when she looked down from the tree she saw the very big, strong, but ugly black bear walking to where her baby squirrel was.

"All the forest animals became excited and began chirping, howling, barking, and screeching.

"Big Bear slowly walked to the baby squirrel and with one gulp had the squirrel in his mouth, and then he slowly began to claw and climb his way up the tree. As he clawed up the trunk of the tree passing one branch then another then another, the birds flew away and the possums, squirrels, and other tree dwellers scampered or jumped to other nearby trees and far away from Big Bear.

"Big Bear reached a place in the tree where three strong branches came together, and there with great care he slowly opened his mouth and the baby squirrel fell out safe and sound.

"Mother Squirrel sat stunned in silence as Big Bear retreated down the tree to the ground below and slowly walked away.

"Sometime later Mother Squirrel reported to the forest animals that she saw Big Bear resting peacefully in the forest under one of the big trees.

"'It seemed so funny just seeing him resting there under this tree! Why, he looked almost like all the other animals in the forest. All of sudden, I saw a small butterfly flutter by and rest on Big Bear's brown ear and Big Bear twitched his ear and the butterfly flew away only to land on his nose. Big Bear began to chuckle and seemed delighted by the playful, soft touch of the butterfly. For the longest time, Big Bear rested there playing and enjoying the company of the butterfly.'

"All the animals in the forest were shocked and then Mother Squirrel said something even more shocking: 'And you want to know something else? Big Bear now has brown fur and is no longer black.'

"'Oh, you are in need of glasses,' Grey Wolf said. 'A bear never changes the color of his fur.'

"All the other animals quickly agreed.

"The next day, Young Doe got caught in a hunter's trap and the poor animal was crying and crying for help. Suddenly, Big Bear appeared and Young Doe began to cry with fear for she knew she was Big Bear's next meal.

"'What is wrong, Young Doe?' asked strong, ugly Big Bear.

"Young Doe was too frightened to answer.

"'Oh, you got yourself caught. Well that can easily be taken care of,' said strong, ugly Big Bear as he pried the trap open with his big paws.

"Young Doe, still in pain, slowly pulled her leg from the trap but could not run away, so she curled up waiting for Big Bear to take a bite of her.

"'If you lick the wound it will heal faster, but with your small tongue you will be hurting for a long time. Let me lick it for you. My tongue is bigger and wider.'

"Young Doe closed her eyes and began to pray to Saint Francis, for she knew she would be with him soon in heaven.

"But all Big Bear did was lick her wound softly and when he thought she was better he walked away.

"Several days later, Young Doe was walking through the forest telling everyone that she saw Big Bear, and his fur was not black as before or brown as Mother Squirrel had said, but light brown, and his eyes seemed to sparkle with gentleness.

"'That cannot be,' said Grey Wolf. 'Bears just don't change, and once a bear is ugly and hungry he is always ugly and hungry. I suggest we be careful; he may be trying to trick us.'

"All the animals in the forest strongly agreed with Grey Wolf.

"A week later there was a big rainstorm in the forest and many of the trees lost their branches and countless bushes were uprooted and dragged away by the flooding river. Many of the smaller animals that lived in burrows and holes in the ground were without homes, shelter, or protection because the rain had flooded their burrows. Among the animals that lost their home was Mother Rabbit who had just given birth to seven babies. With no place to go, the mother gathered her small family and began to cry, for she knew that during the night she and her babies would most likely die from the bad weather.

"Suddenly, Big Bear came walking toward her and Mother Rabbit sprung to her feet and was ready to run when she realized she could not leave her babies. Bravely she stood by her babies and knew that she and her family were to be the bear's next meal.

"'What seems to be the problem?' Big Bear asked.

"Mother Rabbit was too frightened to reply.

"'What beautiful babies you have,' Big Bear said as he lowered his head toward the baby rabbits. 'You should take them home before some mean animal eats them.'

"'We have no home,' Mother Rabbit said in a shaking and fearful voice. 'The rains flooded our house and we are homeless, and I do not have the energy to burrow another hole.'

"'Well, that can be taken care of very quickly,' Big Bear said as he promptly began to dig a deep hole by a big tree.

"When he had finished, he sat and said, 'There, you have a new home,' and with his big claw he gently pushed the babies inside and bid the Mother Rabbit 'Good day' as he slowly walked into the forest.

"About a week later, Mother Rabbit was running through the forest and she found herself directly in front of Big Bear. She was totally surprised to see how good he looked, and that his fur was not black or brown or light brown, but beige—it became him! Even more surprising was that Big Bear looked totally handsome.

"She stood on her hind legs and said, 'Mister Big Bear, I want to thank you for being so kind. Many of us never knew you to be so nice and kind and I am so happy I was one of those proven wrong.'

"'But Mother Rabbit, I was always what I am,' Big Bear said and he turned and slowly lumbered away.

"She ran back and told the other forest animals what she had experienced.

"'There must be something wrong with your eyes,' Grey Wolf declared. 'An ugly bear is always an ugly bear. His fur may change colors but he is still ugly and that makes him mean. Now I know he is planning to trick us, so I suggest we all be very, very careful.'

"All the animals in the forest enthusiastically agreed with Grey Wolf.

"Sometime later, two brothers were playing by the river. Accidentally the older brother fell against the younger brother and the younger brother fell into the river. The older brother yelled for help but by the time the villagers heard his cries his brother was swept downriver.

"All the villagers were screaming and yelling as they ran along the riverbanks trying to find a way to get to the little boy.

"All at once a woman cried, 'Look! The big bear is swimming to the boy. Oh, God, he is going to kill the boy.'

"Immediately some of the men ran home and got their rifles as the other villagers threw stones and sticks at the big bear, but the bear ignored everyone as he continued to swim quickly to the young brother. Finally, he reached the boy and opening his mouth wide he caught the boy's arm and turning began swimming to the bank of the river. After reaching the riverbank, he slowly and carefully pulled the frightened, crying boy onto the bank and leisurely sauntered away.

"The villagers ran to the boy and quickly took him to the hospital where he was declared well and the doctors sent him home.

"Two weeks later, the boy took his older brother by the hand and led him into the forest to show him something.

"'Come here, brother, let me show you my new friend.'

"Suddenly, the big bear came running out of the bushes.

"'Oh my goodness! Run!' the older brother shouted as he turned to run.

"'No, brother, this is my new friend,' the younger brother said as he ran to the big bear and patted him on the head.

"The older brother froze with terror.

"'Come here, brother. Come and pet my furry friend. Have you ever seen such a beautiful snow-white bear like him before?'

"The older brother could not answer him, for he had never seen such a big, mean, ugly, black bear in all his life."

The "Righter of Wrongs" leaned forward in his chair and looked at the two young boys.

"Do you know the message of this story?"

They both shrugged their shoulders and shook their heads.

"Well, to those who received no help or kindness from the big bear he was still big, mean, ugly, and black, but to those who received help, he was brown, light brown, beige, or pure white. Do you know why? Well, you have to learn something from this story and I will tell you. I will repeat an old, old sayings that goes: 'Beauty is in the eye of the beholder.' That lady you were making fun of is to some people helpful, kind, considerate, respectful, and loving and may be very smart. To those people she is beautiful because they see beyond the face and the bad eyes. I would bet to some people she is the greatest person in the world, which is more than what I can say of you two guys at this moment."

The "Righter of Wrongs" sat back in his chair and looked at the boys over his eyeglasses.

"There is also an old Italian saying that goes, *Ogni scarafaggio sembra bello allo propria madre*—Even a cockroach is beautiful to his mother." With a smile on his face, the "Righter of Wrongs" said, "Always look beyond what is before you. So now, did we learn a lesson today?"

"Yeah, Dad."

"Yes."

"Good. You're both grounded this weekend."

"But, Daddy…."

"No 'but Daddy' allowed. You were wrong and you are both lucky I did not tan your backsides. Now go do some homework or studying and do not be a bother to your mother or me."

The two boys slowly walked away, then stopped.

"Dad, is that one of the stories your Nonna told you?"

"No. This one I made up," the father answered with a broad smile on his lips.

The boys turned to leave the room as they heard their father continue, "But it sure did sound a lot like one of her stories."

◆ THE JOY YOU GIVE GOD ◆

Every Friday during Lent all the students in our school would go to church for the Stations of the Cross. The Stations of the Cross are represented by small plaques that adorn the side walls of all Catholic churches and depict various incidents of Christ's way to Golgotha. When "doing the Stations," each station is visited by a small procession led by a priest and three altar boys. Two altar boys carried candles and the other altar boy who always walked between the two candle bearers would carry a cross. For some unknown reason the cross bearer was always taller than the candle bearers. The congregation participates by responding to the priest from a small book that had all the prayers and responses in it.

There are fourteen depictions and each one is accompanied with prayers. The prayers tell Jesus of our sorrow at His Agony and Suffering for our sake and with prayers for forgiveness, of thanksgiving, and of praise for His dying to make us all become Christians.

After all fourteen Stations are visited, the priest leads the congregation in Benediction. The Eucharistic Body of Christ is placed in a gold and beautifully ornamented vessel called a *monstrance* for all to adore and worship, with incense, hymns, and prayers. Finally, the congregation is blessed with the Body of Christ.

The Stations had a strong hold on me. In my early years of school, I believe I enjoyed the repeated standing and kneeling that are a part of this devotion. Also in my early years I loved Benediction and the Eucharistic hymn *Tantum*

Ergo which was sung in Latin and only at Benediction. It was written by Saint Thomas Aquinas and it is a beautiful hymn. I just enjoyed the flow of the Latin words of this hymn, which sounded a lot like Italian. When I sang this hymn, I felt I was so smart and proud of myself because I was able to speak Latin. My joy at singing this hymn always prompted me to sing it loudly; so loud that one Friday, Mother Mary Edward took me from my second-grade pew at the back of the church, which was where all lower classes sat, and led me to the first seat in the first row which was reserved for the eighth-grade boys. Needless to say I walked proudly for weeks and I felt ever so "grown-up." Next to coffee with Nonna and unraveling *bracciole,* that moment was up there.

When I got to third or fourth grade, the Stations gave me the opportunity to become more of a participant in that long-ago Good Friday. Every time we came to a Station where a new person entered the Way to the hill, my imagination came into play, and I began to see these people and the way they dressed, walked, and even how they were perspiring. On most of these Lenten Fridays, Nonna would stop her housework and come to church for "the Stations" and then she, my cousins, and I would all walk home together. For some unknown reason one particular Friday, only Nonna and I walked home together, and as we walked I became very talkative. I mentioned how I would imagine the people in the Stations and I told her of the great joy I got out of imagining these people.

Nonna appeared stunned.

"And just how do you picture these people?" she asked with a degree of disbelief and curiosity in her voice.

"Oh, different ways."

"Tell me…tell me how does Saint Veronica look to you?"

"I see her as a little girl with long black hair, nice big dark eyes. She is tanned from the sun and she has nice white teeth. Her face is round but not fat, it is a small face. She is short and delicate. She looks like one of the girls from the eighth grade in my school. For some reason I don't think too many people like Veronica. I think she had to be very tough because she pushed her way through the crowd; even pushed the tall Roman soldiers out of her way. She might be a little thick headed, like I am. She is wearing a pretty white cloth over her head and she is wearing a gray dress with a piece of rope for a belt. She has open sandals and because it is hot she has sweat on her face but still she is pretty."

"Vincenzo, you surprise me. I never thought you had such a nice and beautiful imagination," Nonna said, sounding very pleased with me.

Suddenly her walk put on a new and different stride. It was more like a strut and her head was held high with shoulders thrown back, and soon a happy but small grin spread across her lips. She was proud, and I was surprised by her pride, and because she was happy I became equally happy.

"Now tell me about Saint Simon of Cyrene. You know he was from Africa?"

"Yes, and I picture him tall, taller than you, Nonna, taller than anyone I ever met. He is really dark and his skin makes his eyes and teeth whiter. He has a lot of black, curly hair. He has a mustache and a nice short beard that a barber must have trimmed or he, maybe, trimmed himself. He has big, big muscles, big shoulders and big hands. He also is wearing open sandals and has a long, yellow robe and a bright-green cloak over his robe and for some reason he looks like he is mad. I don't think he wants to help Jesus. I think he is mad because he wanted to do something else—something that is important to him."

"You see all this?"

"Yes, Nonna. Is it wrong?"

"Well, no, I don't think so. Of course not! Something this nice can never be wrong."

We walked a bit further in silence.

"I really don't think there is anything wrong in your thinking or what you are doing, Vinzee," she said, thinking aloud to help convince herself and me.

We continued walking along the street, again in silence. My small hand was smothered by her big, wrinkled hard-worked hand.

"When I was a little girl I use to put myself in the Stations."

"What?" I said in surprise and became instantly excited that I had done something that was near to what she had done.

"I would pretend I was standing along the street as Jesus went by carrying His Cross."

"Really?" I said in wonder and immediately resolved that I was going to try doing the same thing the next time we did the Stations.

"Yes. You see, I always wanted to be there. Now, in my old age…" She continued with a sigh, "I think we were all there that day, if not in body then in thought. We are always with Jesus when He carries His Cross."

"I don't understand," I said, disappointed that I could not grasp what apparently was very important.

She laughed and in between her laughter she said, "I guess it is a bit too much for you to understand. You see, because Jesus was dying for all our sins we were there. The whole world—the world that passed before Him, the world that He was living in, and the world to come. All time was there. Do you understand, now?"

"I think so," I replied, hoping that what I understood was what she meant for me to understand.

"Yet, pretending that I was there made me so happy, because more than anything I always wanted to be there on Good Friday."

"Why would you want to be a part of that day, Nonna?" I asked, always feeling that Good Friday was not really a "good" day.

"Because everything that was happening that day was being done for me. When I did this it made me feel closer to Jesus and I understood and felt His love for me better."

She coughed softly and swallowed hard to clear her throat.

"You see, most people who do the Stations only think of the sadness, but when I imagined that I was there I felt the strength, the love, and the joy that was also there. I felt the Father and the Holy Ghost and all the heavens."

Her steps became automatic and very precise. She was remembering, reliving that time. "A lot of good things happened that day. It was a busy day because Jesus helped, converted, and saved many people. Look at the people who were there. Veronica got a picture of Christ on her veil, and she became a saint; Simon helped carry the sins of the world, and he became a saint. The Holy Women who cried received a prediction and a warning; I bet they were saved when Jerusalem was destroyed. All the Holy Ladies who stood with Mary became saints. Our dear Mother, Mary, understood what Gabriel and Simeon had said to her and she was thankful. Look at all the soldiers and bystanders who were converted that day, and then there was the Good Thief who became the first saint. So when we do the Stations, we imagine the people there and we have the chance to be become holy and saints."

I must have had my "you got to be crazy" look on my face, because Nonna looked at me and smiled widely.

"Maybe I should tell you a story and that may make you understand. When I was a little girl my Momma, your *Nonna grande,* great-grandmother, told me a story about this little girl who loved to do the Stations. This little girl would do them every time she went into a church but she always needed to do them by herself because she was afraid people would not understand what happened when she did the Stations. You see, every time she came to the Fourth Station where Jesus meets Mary, she would cry. She felt so sorry that Jesus was suffering so much and it made her sad that Mary, who was so good, had to live to see this bad thing happen to her Son and to the Son of God. The girl was saddened that Mary had to endure this sad goodbye. She would just stand there and cry and cry; sometimes for a long, long time and sometimes she would sob out loud. For years every time she did the Stations this would happen.

"Well, eventually this little girl grew up and she stopped going to church, and stopped praying, and soon she stopped believing in God and became a bad girl doing very bad things. Her sins made God very unhappy. She stayed this way for many, many years. She never changed, never prayed, never went back to God.

"Finally she died and she went to her judgment before God. Now when we die and go to our judgment, all the saints and angels, especially our Guardian Angel, attend our judgment. Those saints who became our friends because we had prayed to them, along with all our relatives and friends who we have prayed for, come to our judgment and they act as our witnesses. The saints and all the people tell God the Father what they know we did that was good or bad and how hard we tried or did not try to be good.

"Now when this poor girl died, God the Father, who had been made unhappy with her life, remembered all the bad things she did.

"Saint Veronica and Saint Simon, the two saints of the Stations of the Cross, told God the Father of all the times she did the Stations when she was young, but God was still disappointed because the girl had become such a great sinner over the years. What good she had done when she was young was washed away because her sins were heavier than all her prayers. He found it hard to forgive her and He was about to condemn her to hell, when suddenly Mary stood up and said she had just remembered something important, and asked God if He could call a recess for a few moments. God, who is always so very busy, didn't really want to have a recess, but because He is a just and merciful God, and because Mary asked for a recess, He declared a small recess.

"Mary jumped up from her seat and rushed out of God's Judgment Room and across several clouds to her house. When she got inside her house, she began opening boxes and containers and began moving things around. She was looking for something and was near tears because she could not find what she was looking for, when suddenly she came across a big old rusty, dirty trunk. She opened the trunk and began digging down deep inside until she found what she was looking for, and then she quickly ran back to the Judgment Room.

"God the Father was sitting tapping his fingers on the arm of His throne. It was obvious He had grown impatient and wanted to go about doing godly things.

"'Almighty One, I have something that I think You should see,' Mary said, breathing heavily, and she held out to show God and everyone an old dirty and soiled cloth that was falling apart in her hand.

"God looked at the cloth in bewilderment and all the angels and saints in the room looked at the piece of cloth in disgust. Slowly Mary began unwrapping the old cloth and as she unfolded the old, dirty cloth it broke apart. Finally she uncovered a handful of precious diamonds, which she showed to everyone in the room. All the saints and angels and others in the room sighed with wonder because the diamonds were so big, so beautiful, and so bright. They sparkled so intensely that many of the happy souls in the Judgment Room had to shade their eyes from the blinding brightness.

"'I remember this girl as a child and as a young lady,' Mary said. 'Each and every time she would come to the Station where Jesus and I met, she would cry. These many diamonds are her many tears. Her tears were so valuable and so filled with compassion and sorrow for what Jesus and I had suffered that they turned into diamonds shaped like tears.'

"Everyone in the Throne Room let out a cheer and applauded loudly, and God the Father grew so pleased that He forgave the girl and didn't send her to hell."

Nonna stopped walking and looked down at me.

"Do you understand what I am trying to say now, Vinzee?"

"Kind of," I said still not too sure of having the meaning of the story.

"Well let me talk a little more."

She turned and with slow steps she continued down the street. Wetting her lips she continued, "Veronica showed courage when she wiped Jesus' face. Here was a little girl pushing her way through a mad crowd, shoving her way past many angry people just to do a kind and nice thing for Jesus. Do we have the courage to do that for Jesus? Do we help others who need our help when no one else is willing to help? Do we do nice and kind things for Jesus?"

She cleared her throat.

"Simon of Cyrene had to do Jesus' work. Jesus was supposed to carry His own Cross, but Simon carried the Cross for Him. You know they don't tell us how long Simon did carry the Cross. He could have carried it the rest of the way, all of the way up to Calvary, or he could have just carried it for a short time. It really doesn't matter because the important thing is he was doing Jesus' work, and that is what we have to do because we are now supposed to be Jesus in our time on earth. We are supposed to be doing His work. So do we help Jesus in the world? Do we carry our cross each day? Are we doing what is expected of us?"

She stopped talking and as we continued walking we remained silent. I watched her face, knowing more was coming and I knew she was thinking.

She soon continued. "Now when you put yourself into the Stations you become part of what was. You are there and you are a part of it all and by doing this you can feel and see many other things. It is good to do this. When you do your Bible History in school or when you read the Bible it is always good to put yourself in the stories. You come to live the Gospels and the Bible that way. You don't have to have an important part. You could be just watching. The important thing is that you feel and understand what is going on and what is happening."

"Do you do this, Nonna?"

"Yes, and I have been to the parting of the Red Sea, the walking on water, the Last Supper, even the coming of the Holy Spirit."

I grew excited and a thousand stories from the Scriptures came to my mind that I knew I wanted to become a part of and I wanted to go off to be alone, and to think of these stories and find myself in them.

"I think I got it now, Nonna, and I'm going to do it, and I can't wait until I start," I said excitedly, "but before I can do that I have to think about all those questions you asked and see if I am doing those things and then later, I'm going to spend a lot of time going into the Bible and learn how to live in it."

Nonna smiled to herself, pleased that she had taught a new and good lesson. We continued home in silence, each of us thinking our own and different thoughts.

As we neared home, I said, "Nonna, what do you think Mary did with those diamonds?"

"Oh, I don't know. What do you think she did with them?"

I smiled, for I was happy that Nonna was giving me an opportunity to be clever and smart like her.

"I think she threw them out the window of the Judgment Room into the night sky and that is why we have twinkle, twinkle little stars."

Nonna laughed aloud. Her entire body shook with joy.

"Good, Vincenzo, very good." Her loud laughter turned to a chuckle.

"That is something you would say, Nonna."

"Yes, I know," she beamed happily and squeezed my hand slightly.

We both settled down with wide smiles that continued until we arrived at home. As we walked up the front steps to the house, Nonna said, "You know, Vinzee, your image of Saint Simon is the way I see him. Isn't that good that we both see him that way? I like what you are doing. It is good, but remember what I just told you about the girl who cried. She felt the sorrow that Jesus and Mary had when they met. If you are getting joy from using your imagination, this is a gift for you, but try to remember to feel something for God in your imagination, for then you will learn the joy you give God."

◆ THE WHITE LILY ◆

I had to repeat the first grade because I could not speak English very well. It was inevitable, for when Nonna spoke English she spoke with an Italian accent. I mimicked her and pronounced my words as she did. Of course, the fact that Sister Mary Magdalene spoke with an Irish accent did not help the situation much. I had a hard time understanding words like "Lass" and "Laddie," or "'Tis a great morn'…'tis indeed," and "The top of the morn' to ye…"

I also believe there was another reason for my being held back. Sister Mary Magdalene was a very, very young nun who had not yet taken her final vows to religious life. She was very, very pretty and one day I proposed marriage to her by saying, "When I grow up I am going to marry you." Many years later when I met Sister again, the only thing she remembered about me was that I was the only male who had proposed to her.

When Nonna heard that I was held back because of my English, she pulled me aside and began to correct the situation. "Vinzee, you are an American. I am Italian-Italian. (She was not yet a naturalized American citizen). Your mother and father are Italian-Americans. You are American-American. It is good to speak Italian, that is a great privilege given to you by God, and you speak Italian to me and others from the 'old country' because you are being polite and do not want us to feel stupid. You must begin listening to the good Sisters and speak good English, so you may become a good American."

So the next year I began listening to "the good Sisters" and began to speak with an Irish accent which amused others, especially "the good sisters," who then allowed me to pass to the second grade.

One day during my second year in first grade, I was summoned to Mother Mary Edward's office. Now, you have to know that being called to Mother's office was a rare and dangerous thing. First of all, it could mean you were to be severely corrected for having done something unspeakable. It also could be bad news from home or some other familiar place. It could even mean you were to learn something about yourself you did not know, such as having been seen doing something unkind or unchristian. Simply stated, to be summoned to Mother's office was a notice of pending death.

Her office was the only room in the entire school which had linoleum flooring, window shades, and curtains. Her linoleum floor was so highly polished that the ceiling lights reflected brightly off it. In comparison to the rest of the school, it was like being summoned to the palace of the queen. Many things raced through my mind as I walked up the steps to the sacred domain, and by the time I arrived I knew that whatever was wrong, I was set to cry loud and long.

When I arrived, Mother simply and without any care announced that I was being considered to lead our October procession to honor Christ the King of Peace. I knew this was an honor and I immediately got excited, but when I heard that two other boys from my class were being considered, my excitement ebbed. However, I returned to my class with a smile, for I was sure I was not to be chosen. One of the boys lived in our parish rectory and his Aunt Jenny was housekeeper and cook for the priests. The other boy was the son of one of the richest families in our parish. I acknowledged that my chances were slim. Besides, to be chosen meant I was to wear a blonde, curly wig, a long, white and gold polka-dot dress, a heavy, metal crown of great value (even if it was fake), and a long flowing cape carried by two page boys who were equally hideously dressed. Who wanted to walk around the neighborhood and its many city blocks looking like a girl?!

In all honesty, the first time I saw the procession and the boy who represented Christ the King, I wondered if Christ really looked anything like the representation. Even in heaven, I cannot imagine Him being represented this way, but it was how the Franciscan Sisters in our school saw Him.

I left school that day a bit at ease and unconcerned as to whether or not I would be chosen. When I walked into the house, however, it seemed I could not announce quickly enough the idea that I was being considered for this honor, and immediately the house went into complete joy. Nonna went into absolute overjoy. I had never seen her so happy and excited, and this pleased me so much that I overlooked my own conclusions. In fact, I was kind of regretting to tell her of the other boys, but I knew I had to tell her of my slim chance.

"I'm excited that Mother Edward told me, but when she mentioned who the other two boys were I knew I would not be chosen."

"And why not? You are as good as they are."

"To you and our family I am, but not to Father Casago. He will pick Aunt Jenny's nephew or the richest boy in the school."

Nonna stopped doing her cooking and looked at me. I could see from the expression on her face that she agreed with me. If I were chosen, it would be a great honor for Nonna and my family; for that reason, I would want to be picked, but we were just plain, ordinary people.

Nonna broke her stare and returned to her cooking.

"Well," she finally said, "it is in the hands of God."

"Well, if it is in the hands of God, there will have to be a miracle for me to be picked."

"Do not treat God's will so lightly. I am sure Father Casago will pick the right boy and the one that God wants chosen. Father is familiar with the presence of God's will. He is aware that the hand of God is on his shoulder and he will do the will of God. He knows his soul will be in grave danger if he does not do God's will. A priest who fails to do the will of God and does his own will is not a servant of God but of his own will. He becomes a sinner and maybe a bigger sinner than us."

I looked blankly at her and I was sure she knew I did not understand what she had just said.

"You are confused and I again have spoken over your head. I am sorry. Believe me, whoever is chosen will be picked by the will of God. You know now that we're talking about the will of God. I remember a story about a man who felt unworthy, yet was chosen by God. Let us talk about him. Go get the things for coffee."

I quickly gathered the cups, paper napkins, spoons, milk, and Karo.

She went for the coffee, and with the pot in her hand she stood waiting for all the things I had gathered to be put in place. She then expertly poured our coffee.

After sitting down, she began to stir her coffee, and the usual cling-clang sound of the circling spoon against the coffee cup filled the room. I watched, as I always did, mesmerized by her actions, and not realizing that while she was doing this she was creating the story in her mind.

After taking a sip of hot coffee, she began. "Many years ago, there was a young man whose wife had died and left him with four sons and two daughters. In the Jewish faith, men and women—really boys and girls—married young. The man in our story may have been around 30 years old."

"Nonna, that is not young!"

"Oh, yes it is. Wait until you become 30 and you'll see how young it is. Let us get back to the story. Now in his village was a young lady who was of marrying age. She was about fourteen. She had thought of being a virgin all her life, but when marriage was suggested to her she knew God had other plans for her. In the Jewish custom of that time, a matchmaker, similar to the matchmaker in my village in Italy who matched me with my first husband, Lorenzo Garnella, was hired to find the perfect husband for the young virgin whose name was Mary. Well, this matchmaker presented three good men for Mary to pick, but she just could not decide who would be the better husband for her. So the matchmaker went to the Temple, and the Temple priest suggested leaving the choice in God's hands.

"Now the three men were all perfect. The first man worked for the Temple priest as a janitor and everyone believed he was the perfect husband for the young Mary. The second man was the son of a rich merchant who had several grape vineyards, date trees, and orange groves. The third man was our widower and he was a simple carpenter who helped people live comfortably. Of the three men, he had the least to offer Mary and was not the most likely to be chosen. I do not know the names of the other men, but I do know that the widower's name was Joseph. Of the three candidates, he was the least likely to be chosen. The Temple priest asked each of the candidates to come to the Temple and pray, and as they each left the Temple, the priest took their walking staffs and told them to return the next day. The priest then placed each of the staffs on the altar of the Temple and went to bed. The next day all three men returned to the Temple. With the Temple priest, they went to the altar. Two staffs were as they had been the night before but one had a white lily wrapped around it. No one knew how the flower got there, but they all agreed that this was a sign of who the husband was to be. The staff belonged to the widower with the children, the one least likely to be chosen."

She stopped speaking and took a long drink of coffee.

"Is that a true story, Nonna?" I asked with certain doubt.

"Yes, of course. A great Italian writer wrote a book about it and the whole world heard this story."

"The whole world knows the story?"

"Yes."

"How come I just heard it?"

"You just heard it because it was the will of God for you to hear it now, and for you to learn that sometimes when things are out of our hands we must remember they are in the hands of God."

I knew I had been very gently corrected and needed to be still. We continued our coffee in silence.

Nonna finally finished her coffee, and gathering her spoon and cup, walked to the sink. She began washing them in hot sudsy water.

"So you have learned something new," Nonna commented, "and that is always a good thing. We must always learn something new every day of our lives. So, like my story, we will leave the choice of who will be Christ the King of Peace in the October procession to God."

For the next two days upon arriving home from school, Nonna would ask if the announcement had been made. Every day I would change the subject, because I did not want to see her disappointment.

On the third day, I finally returned to the story of Joseph and asked her, "What other story did 'some great Italian writer' write about Joseph?"

"I remember in his book that the great Italian writer tells how Joseph was a good carpenter. All the furniture in their house was made by him. His work was so good that he was in great demand by many of his neighbors, rich and poor. In fact, one rich man who had trouble with his leg asked Joseph to make a stool for him so he could rest his foot on it. Joseph made a beautiful stool. He carved flowers and trees on the side and made the wood smooth and perfect. It was the most beautiful piece of furniture in the rich man's house. Not long after that, the rich man died and his son kept the stool because it was such a beautiful, artistic piece of furniture. Many years later the rich man's son invited Jesus to visit his home. The man who invited Jesus to his house presented Jesus with the stool to rest His feet. As soon as Jesus' foot touched the stool, He recognized it and smiled warmly as He remembered His noble, gentle, and earthly father. While He was resting, a woman came in and with tears in her eyes she anointed Jesus' feet with perfume and wiped His feet dry with her long, black hair. Everyone was disturbed by what the woman did but Jesus reassured them by saying that she was preparing Him for His death.

"How did Jesus know that Joseph made the stool?"

"Jesus knows everything, and besides, the stool was made because God willed it to be made and to be used by His Son. God always presents us with things to do, and all we need is to accept the gift He presents to us, and then we are doing His will."

She walked to the gas range, picked up her big wooden spoon, and began stirring her homemade soup. It was a big pot so I became curious.

"Nonna, you made a lot of soup. Are you expecting company?"

"No, Mrs. Love has a cold so I decided she could use some good soup. Besides, she likes Italian food and likes my cooking."

Mrs. Love was our next-door neighbor and someone we liked, and who also liked us. She was an elderly woman. She was a rarity because she was not Italian in a mostly Italian neighborhood, and wasn't Catholic in a completely Catholic neighborhood. When Mrs. Love's sons went into the service, Nonna felt it was her duty to tend to the elderly lady. Soon food from our table was shared with Mrs. Love and leftover food from many meals were given to her. Every once in a while, Mrs. Love would ask me into her house to get the dishes or pots that were given to her and return them to Nonna's kitchen.

Mrs. Love's house was so unlike our house. The one thing so different in Mrs. Love's house was it never smelled of anything. It had no odor of baked bread or gravy or cookies or cake. She would always give me a nickel or dime and I would hurry home, and when I entered the house I would take a deep breath and thank God for my warm smelling house.

Nonna stopped stirring the soup and turned to me with a wooden spoon in her hand. Smiling, she said, "Joseph one day made Mary a long wooden spoon; it was the first long wooden spoon ever made. He did this so she would not get burned while stirring the family dinner. Ever since that day many wooden spoons have been made like the one he made. There is a legend that the spoon Joseph made is still somewhere in the world and has been used by many great saints to do the will of God. Today, they say, it is used to stir the souls and minds of people."

Nonna placed her wooden spoon on the kitchen table.

"Do you know how important a wooden spoon is to a cook?"

"No, but I know you and a lot of mothers and grandmothers have one."

"It is important because without a spoon, no gravy, soup, or dinner would be made correctly. A cook would not be able to taste the food to see what else was needed to make it better and tastier. It protects the cook and is the most important thing in the kitchen."

She walked quickly to the cupboard and reached for her favorite large, round bowl and carried it to the porcelain kitchen table. She went to the gas range, lugged the big pot of soup to the table, and placed it beside the bowl. She began ladling the soup.

"Now, I will hold the door for you when you carry this to Mrs. Love. Tell her I said this will make her feel better. Do not forget to tell her we are praying that she gets better, and do not be ignorant by not saying you wish her to get better."

I carefully picked up the bowl, which was extremely warm, and hurried behind Nonna as she opened the doors to the house. Once outside, she knocked on Mrs. Love's door and retreated quickly into our house. For some unknown reason, when I or one of my cousins had to deliver things to our neighbors, Nonna would never stay to receive any praise or thanks.

I waited for Mrs. Love to open the door. It took her a long time, for she walked with a cane and was never too fast. Meantime, my hands were getting hotter. Soon, the door opened and I presented Mrs. Love with Nonna's homemade chicken soup.

The next day after school, Nonna asked me if a student had been chosen. I told her no announcement was made and quickly said I had to do homework. I didn't want to talk about it or see the look of concern on her face. I raced to the dining table and began to empty my school backpack. I looked at my pile of books and copybooks and slowly began to organize what had to be done. For Religion, I had to study and answer the questions on the Sacraments; for Mathematics, I had to memorize the two times table; for writing, I was to print fifteen words that begin with the letter "V"; and for Grammar, I was to memorize the personal pronouns.

I sat down and began doing my work with great vigor; I wanted to go out and play. About ten minutes into my homework, the phone rang. I knew Nonna would not answer the phone when someone else was home, so I jumped from my chair and ran to the phone. I listened carefully to the voice on the other end of the receiver and then returned the phone to the cradle. I let the flow of pride and happiness flood my ego.

"*Vinzee, che e?*" Who is it?

"It was Mother Mary. She wants to talk to my mother to tell her I was chosen to be Christ the King in the October procession."

I didn't have to turn. I knew Nonna was standing at the doorway to the dining room. I felt her eyes on my back. Finally turning, I found her face wet with tears.

The house went into full drive. Nonna and my mother, with the help of my Aunt Jenny and Aunt Millie, began sewing my white, long pants—my very first pair of long pants. My Aunt Rita bought me a white, long-sleeved shirt— my first ever—and once again my Holy Communion shoes were put to use. At the end of the week, my mother went to the convent to pick up my costume. The wig, crown, polka-dot gown, and cape were in the package. To our surprise, we found a pair of sandals. I immediately became excited because I knew that Saint Francis of Assisi wore them, and I quickly associated myself to this great saint.

Word was sent out to aunts, uncles, cousins, and distant relatives of the great honor bestowed upon our family. On the day of the procession, Nonna's house was packed with family. Of course, there was food and cakes, cookies, and coffee.

After I dressed and made my entrance, I was scooped away by one of my cousins into his automobile and taken to the school. On the way there, my first problem of the day matured. It was October and a cold, damp day. My feet and toes were quickly freezing. I soon forgot about the honor of wearing sandals like Saint Francis of Assisi.

The procession proceeded down many streets of our parish, and I became colder with each step. It was very windy and the cape continued to tug at my long dress and soon the front of the dress was pulled almost up to my knees. The wind decided to play with the long, blonde, curly wig, and by the time I got to the church, the wig and crown were far from centered on my head.

Entering the church, I realized that I was not going to find relief from the cold, for our church never had any heat. Sometimes it was colder inside the church than outside. I proceeded up the center aisle and suddenly began to wonder if God would recognize who I was, for I knew I was in a shambles. Then I glanced off to the right and there stood the statue of Saint Joseph with a white lily wrapped around his staff. With a lot of sympathy and understanding, I had learned how hard it was to follow the will of God. I further realized that Joseph's life must have been as difficult as mine.

◆ WHAT NONNA TAUGHT ME ◆

It was one of those long days—a school day that seemed without end. I struggled through the day to final dismissal. I walked regimentally in the "Bridge Street Line" with my class to Twenty-Fourth Street. After the line was released, I walked on the park side of the street. The sounds of the breeze pushing gently through the leaves of the trees made me forget the day, and I stopped and admired the trees around me. The world seemed so big that day. It was full of happenings and I wasn't a part of it. Being a young boy seemed to be the worst thing to be at that moment. As I continued my walk home, I realized the reason for my feeling so down. Sister had told us of the death of a Catholic chaplain in the war and how the family, who lived in our parish, was in mourning. Later, Sister told us about Saint Clare and of her courage protecting her convent and sisters from the barbarians, with her great faith in the Blessed Sacrament. It was then that I became aware of all the courage that was taking place around the world. Men were facing death, dying, and war. Women were also suffering the death and wounds of war. Children had to face life with death, sorrow, and hurt all around them. All I could be, and do, was to be me, which didn't seem like too much to be or do.

As I turned to walk up Dickinson Street, I was soon rid of my day and noticed Nonna walking to our house. She had been to the corner grocery store, for she was carrying several brown bags. I ran to her and took one of the bags, and together we continued home.

"So tell me, Vinzee, what did you learn new today?"

I smiled to myself and told her about Sister telling us the story of Saint Clare.

"Saint Clare was a great saint. She was Saint Francis' close friend. Did you know that she was the fastest woman ever to be made a saint by the Church? She had many special gifts. One of her gifts that I always liked was her ability to be in two places at the same time."

"Really? Are you sure of that Nonna?"

"Of course, I am."

"Now that is something I would like to do."

"Why would you like to do that?"

"I could be in school and be with you at the same time."

"And what would that accomplish? You would learn nothing from school because half your mind would be there, and you would be no company to me because half your mind would not be with me."

I did not reply because I knew she was correct.

We entered the house and went directly to the back kitchen.

"Perhaps," she continued, "you just like to be nosey."

I smiled.

She laughed.

"Besides, God only grants this special gift to those who will use it wisely, or when He wants to make something known to others."

"What do you mean, Nonna?"

"God used Saint Clare's gift to show the nuns in her convent that she was special. It made Saint Clare appreciate God, for He blessed her with another great gift which she accepted to glorify God. She had no selfish reason. Do you understand, now?"

"Yes." I responded with some regret, for I still thought it would be fun to be in two places at the same time. I knew I had been corrected, so I decided to change the subject.

I said quickly, "Sister said that Saint Clare was a courageous woman because she stood up to an army of barbarians."

"I agree, but it was God who scared that evil army."

She began to peel some potatoes which I knew were to make *gnocchi patata*—potato dumplings—one of my favorite homemade Italian macaronis.

"I know that, Nonna," I replied. "But still, for a lady to do that took courage."

"Every person has his or her own courage, and sometimes courage comes to the surface without our even wanting it. Sometimes it is a little baby voice and sometimes it is a lion's roar. Courage is a virtue from God."

"There is a lot of courage around the world," I stated with regret.

"Yes, there is." Nonna stopped peeling and looked at me for a long time. I knew she was reading me, and I knew she saw something was bothering me.

"Courage shows itself in many ways. I think to be able to stand on stage and sing, like Caruso did or Sinatra does, takes courage. Don't you think?"

"Of course," I replied.

"And assisting at Mass as an altar boy, like you do, takes courage. Don't you agree?"

"No."

"Well, think of it this way, Vinzee, if you did not say your Latin correctly, the Mass would be incorrect and a bit less pleasing to God. And if you did not move when you were suppose to or do what you were suppose to do, then Father would not be able to continue the Mass."

"Now I see what you mean," I said softly.

"Sometimes admitting we are wrong is a sign of courage. Sometimes doing the small things in life is a sign of courage."

She gathered the peeled potatoes and put them in a large pot. She quickly carried the pot to the sink and filled it with water. Grabbing a *mapeen* dish cloth, she wiped her hands and tossed it over her shoulder.

"Do we need coffee?"

Without answering, I quickly began gathering cups, spoons, paper napkins, Karo, and milk.

When all was settled and the coffee was poured, she said, "I remember hearing a story by a great Italian writer that would help you understand what I am trying to say. Are you willing to hear that story? Good, because I want to tell it."

"Many years ago there was a young shepherd boy named Aaron. He was only eight years old."

"Like me," I said gladly, and suddenly I was part of the story.

Nonna smiled and continued, "Exactly. Well, Aaron was the youngest shepherd boy in his town, and he only took care of the sheep during the day, because watching sheep at night was for men and too dangerous for a boy."

Nonna went on. "Aaron loved to watch sheep. They were such dumb animals, and their being dumb made them rely on him. This made him feel grown-up and as courageous as any of the other men. Among all his sheep he had a favorite little lamb which he called *Tesoro*."

"Treasure," I again chimed in, for I knew *tesoro* was the Italian word for treasure.

"Yes, this small lamb indeed was a treasure to Aaron because the lamb was so beautiful and because he had become a good companion to the boy. Aaron knew the lamb was special because it never got older. He owned the lamb for five years and still it remained a lamb. It also was a perfect, unblemished lamb. *Tesoro* would sit on Aaron's lap for hours, satisfied with being loved, and Aaron would softly pet the lamb's curly fleece. Aaron prayed that God would always keep his companion a lamb. He knew that a lamb such as *Tesoro*, when grown, would be given to the Temple for sacrifice to God. Though this would have been a great honor, Aaron was too selfish to give his pet to God, so he kept asking God to allow him to keep the only thing in his life that was perfect. He also asked God to bless *Tesoro* to remain special.

"Now one very cold, winter night the Old Shepherd, Adam, told Aaron that he would have to watch sheep with the men because several of the shepherds had gotten sick and could not work. Aaron was so very happy, for he finally was going to be a true shepherd and watch a flock of sheep by night. That night there was a full moon in the sky surrounded by thousands and thousands of bright, twinkling stars. The moon was so bright that it made the trees, bushes, rocks, and hills cast great shadows over the empty land and painted everything else silver blue.

"The night was heavy with silence, and the land seemed to fall into a long, peaceful stillness. There were no sounds of wild animals, and even the sheep were silent.

"When Aaron arrived, he immediately became unsure of himself and grew afraid. The sky was so enormous and so endless. It seemed to be pressing against the earth, causing the vast, barren, open fields to appear humbled and in need of life. He felt small and unimportant. He quickly tucked *Tesoro* close to him and smiled, for instantly he felt a great love from his little lamb.

"The shepherds walked among the sheep, counting them, making certain they were all there before they took their charge of them. When all was done, they gathered their dogs and went to sit around a small fire. They needed to get warm and keep warm. Occasionally, one of the dogs would jump to his feet and run off to gather a wandering sheep or to keep the flock together.

"As night wore on, the colder it became and the more frightened Aaron grew. He did not like being a shepherd at night and envied the other men, for they looked so at ease and unafraid of the darkness, the cold, the silence, and the enormity of everything around them. He wished and prayed for daylight.

"One of the shepherds asked, 'Did you hear that?'

"'Hear what?' another asked.

"'The silence. Listen to how quiet everything is.'

"All the shepherds stood up and looked around. There were no sounds.

"Suddenly, the place where the shepherds were was flooded with a bright light. The light was so intense that many of them covered their eyes. Then the sky opened up and angels appeared over and around them. The angels' voices broke the silence of the cold night with praises and joy. Several of the shepherds fell to the ground in fear, while others stood courageously by questioning their eyes. The angels wore flowing gowns of white, pink, blue, yellow, orange, and lavender. They were like a rainbow. Then one appeared taller and stronger than the others, and he told the shepherds of a baby born in nearby Bethlehem who was wrapped in swaddling clothes. The night was thrown open to great singing and rejoicing. Abruptly, all was still and the shepherds, as if in a daze, gathered their belongings and began to walk to town.

"Adam, the oldest and leader of the shepherds, turned to Aaron and told him he had to stay and watch the sheep. Aaron objected. He was not sure he could watch the sheep, for he was afraid of the enormity of the night and of being left alone. He also wanted to go to Bethlehem, but Adam told him he had to stay. So he got his small friend *Tesoro* and sat on a rock. He wrapped a blanket around himself and the lamb and looked out over the land and into the sky. His heart was still beating from all the excitement of the night and from the fear that came with his being alone. He wanted to be away from shepherding and with the others. He wanted to see the Babe in swaddling clothes and find out what was so special about the Babe. The angels had said a King was born, an Anointed One.

"'And I have to sit here alone,' he said aloud. 'I have to sit here and be lost in this world of big things. I am sure if I was older I would be allowed to go into Bethlehem and see the gift the angels spoke of.'

"A strong gust of wind passed and he became chilled. He snuggled into his blanket and pulled his fluffy lamb friend closer to him for warmth and protection. He heard the sheep in the field; they seemed disturbed. He was filled with fear. The sky and land seemed bigger to him. He didn't want to leave the nice warm fire, but he jumped to his feet with the desire to run away. When he did this, *Tesoro* flew from his lap. As soon as he realized what he had done, he looked down for *Tesoro,* but he was not there. His thought was to run to Bethlehem and get help, but when he looked to Bethlehem he saw a bright star lingering over a hillside. From the hillside, a golden ray came to him and Aaron felt himself being carried off. Soon, he was in a small stable where a cow, oxen, donkey, hen, and small birds had gathered and rested, silently looking at a newborn Babe. Standing over the Babe with eyes of wonder and love were the Babe's mother and father. The stable was blanketed with the feeling of peace, yet outside Aaron could still feel the enormity, fears, and dangers of the world. In contradiction, he sensed the world in complete praise of God. From behind him he heard the steps of the shepherds as they approached the stable. He watched Adam, the oldest, fall to his knees and the others become filled with delight and wonder. A few of his friends had sheep with them and they released them, and the sheep quickly walked into the stable and rested with the other animals.

"Aaron wanted to give the Babe something, but he had nothing to give. Then to his surprise, he watched *Tesoro* walk slowly to the manger and lie timidly beside the Babe. The lamb seemed more perfect—whiter—than ever before and looked more at ease with the Babe than he ever had been with Aaron. With a great deal of humility, Aaron knew he had given his gift. Joy and peace were engraved deeply in his heart.

"There was the sound of a wolf and the barking of a sheep dog, and Aaron found himself running to the herd. He whistled and the herd began to come to him, and then he saw the wolf. Waving his arms and shouting, he ran to the wolf and it quickly raced away.

"It was then that Aaron understood what had taken place."

Nonna took a sip of her coffee, which I knew had cooled, and looked at me.

"Tell me, Vinzee, what do you think happened to Aaron?"

I looked at her for a long time. For some unknown reason I hated this question; yet, I knew I had to answer it.

"He was in two places at the same time."

"Yes. You must remember, with God and for God all things are possible. What is amazing is that God always picks the small and seemingly unimportant to show His greatness."

She rose from her chair and carried her cup to the kitchen sink.

"What else is of importance in the story?" she asked.

I followed her to the sink with my cold coffee. Nonna had left her cup and walked to the table with a wet cloth to wipe the table clean. With regret, I emptied the cup into the drain. I washed my cup with suds and hot water over and over again. I ran the story through my head and found nothing more to learn from it.

"There is nothing more, Nonna,"

"Yes there is. Aaron's courage. Do you remember how he raced after the wolf? Remember how he did not fear the night? Sometimes courage comes to us without thought. Instant courage comes from nowhere, but it is always inside us. We all have courage and we use it often, for we are always fighting *il diavolo,* the Evil One, who has great power and great friends such as selfishness, self-love, comfort, and fear. And sometimes we even have to fight ourselves, and that takes great courage."

She looked at me and smiled.

"Ah, I have spoken over your head. Sorry, but sometimes your Nonna likes to think out loud and make no sense."

I find that hard to believe, I thought.

"And you, Vinzee, don't you think you have courage?"

"Not like the courage I hear about."

"Nonsense, of course you have great courage. Don't you have courage to raise your hand in class to read or answer a question? Don't you have courage to correct yourself when you are about to do wrong? Don't you have courage when you get down on your knees and pray to God?"

"Nonna, those things don't take courage."

"Of course they do! When you raise your hand, others are relying on you to give them knowledge, and if Sister calls on you, you have to have courage to answer. When you want to do something bad and you say no to yourself, isn't that being courageous? When you kneel before your Maker, your God, the mightiest Being and pray, don't you think that takes courage? Of course. So you see, you have courage and you never knew it."

I remained silent and let her words mill around in my head. I soon came to the conclusion that once again Nonna was right; that once again she had made life a bit easier for me. For an instant I became inflated and felt courageous.

"There was one other thing that Aaron did that showed his courage." Seeing no positive reaction, Nonna smiled and continued. "He gave up his lamb, *Tesoro*. Whenever we give something of value away, we are courageous. Courage and hope are twin sisters. When we do something courageous, we hope for the best, and when we hope, we have courage that things will become okay. Understand?"

"I think so."

"Good, so think a little longer, and if you have any problems come and see me."

I knew I was being dismissed, so I left the sink and began to walk out of the back kitchen. Suddenly, curiosity jumped into my head.

"Nonna, the lamb, *Tesoro*, did he become Jesus' friend?"

"All of his life. Do you remember in the story that he never got old? Well, our little lamb stayed young for many, many years. When Mary wanted to make Jesus a cloak, she sheared *Tesoro* and used his fleece to make that garment. It was the same garment the soldiers threw dice for. When Jesus began His public life, *Tesoro* began to age, and when the *Pasqua Ebraica,* Jewish Passover came and Mary and her sisters were preparing for the feast, *Tesoro* came over to Mary. With joy in his eyes, he looked at Mary. She knew that it was time for *Tesoro* to be returned to God, and he became the lamb at the Last Supper."

"That's sad."

"No, it isn't, because God uses all His creation for His purpose. The lamb was used out of love and it fulfilled its purpose on earth. I believe that animals are good and innocent. After all, they are the only creatures created by God on the first days that never sinned against Him. God would never forget His faithful ones. He created everything out of love, and love is never destroyed in the other world. Love is the only virtue we take with us to heaven because it is the only thing we need."

She knocked me off my feet. I had learned so much from her that day, and I knew I had to remember it. Someday I knew I would have to have the courage to tell what Nonna had taught me.

◆ A MOTHER ◆

It was a warm, humid spring day in May—the Monday after my First Holy Communion Day. I had the day off from school in celebration of that blessed occasion. Perhaps it was the excitement of staying home while the rest of the family had to go to school and work that made me wake early. I listened as one by one my aunts and my mother left for the factories to help America win the War. I relaxed even more when I heard my cousins say their loud *Caio,* goodbye, as they left for school. With a small smile on my lips, I settled down in my bed of comfort and delight. I soon began to enjoy the rare silence and peace that always followed the last morning departure. All that seemed to move in the house was silence, and the aroma of morning coffee moved heavily through the downstairs rooms and up to my room.

Still in the limelight of my First Communion, which had left me feeling special and close to Jesus, I decided to spend my day basking in His company. I would do some studying and finally go out to play.

All of a sudden, the aroma of coffee overpowered me. It became a strong beckoning call. I leapt from my bed and walked briskly to the bathroom. I vigorously washed the look of sleep from my face, slowly and carefully brushed my teeth with Colgate, and then decided to cheat a little and use Aunt Rita's Ipana toothpaste to add flavor to my breath. As I brushed my teeth, I remembered Nonna saying that Italians had the most blessed teeth and mouths in the world, because over their teeth passed the best food and wine; in their mouths came the finest language ever spoken to thank God, and from their mouths the best poems were recited and greatest songs sung to praise God. There was no doubt in my mind what she said was true.

When I finished, I wet my hair with water, tried to comb my blond wavy hair, and went back to my bedroom. As I undressed and leisurely dressed, I said my Morning Offering and a quick prayer to my patron saints and other heavenly "Buddies," and then an "Eternal Rest..." for all my dead relatives. Fully dressed, I started down the long hallway to the stairs and recited two quick "Glory Be..." prayers for my family and others in the war. I had grown thirsty from the smell of coffee and was now moving fast, for I was on a quest. I knew waiting for me was my usual breakfast of hard Italian bread with butter to dunk in coffee.

Briskly, I went down the stairs, walked through the living room, passed the dining room table with its constant vigil of burning candles; then the dinette, and into the back kitchen and more coffee with Nonna.

"*Nonna, di buona mattina*," good morning, Grandmother, I said joyfully and with a giant, early-morning smile.

"*Buona mattina a tu*," good morning to you, Nonna said, returning the morning greeting to me after lowering her coffee cup from her lips.

I was shocked to see my Aunt Jenny seated at the table drinking coffee with Nonna.

"*Buona mattina, Zia*," good morning, Aunt, I said quickly to avoid any disrespect or oversight.

"Are you sick, Aunt Jenny?" I continued in English with concern, for my aunt was never one to miss work except for death in the family or serious, serious illness.

"No, Vince, I'm going with you and Grandmom to the viewing."

What viewing?

"Who died?" I asked them now aware they were both in black dresses. I braced myself for a shock.

"Commah Seppina's grandson. Remember, I told you?" Nonna said with a bit of sadness in her voice and a touch of grief on her face.

With all the excitement of Holy Communion, I had forgotten Nonna and my mother telling me of the six-month-old baby's death.

"I forgot," I said quickly.

Though this was a sad thing and I felt badly for the family, it was not a horrific ordeal for me, because I knew the baby was in heaven, and also because from early childhood my cousins and I were made accustomed to deaths, wakes, and funerals. The adults in my family never tried to make death something to be feared or dreaded. They made us aware of death and its ceremonies. It was a part of life and always encouraged us to mourn respectfully whenever death came, and, in duty of love, to remember the dead in prayers. My family was so large and extended that it was near impossible not to be touched with death at least two or three times a year. Besides, we were at war and telegrams of killings from the War Department to our family, extended family, neighbors, and friends were a common occurrence. Although we lived life appreciatively, we respectfully knew death was near and part of living.

So after bread and butter and coffee, I went to my room and dressed in something more presentable. With resignation, I surrendered my plans for the day and went with Nonna and Aunt Jenny to the viewing.

Let me explain what the word *commah* means. It really is *commare*. Today among Italians and others it has a touch of mockery to it. It now implies being old fashioned, old European, and overly simplistic, but in my youth it was a word of great respect. First off, it was a title given to one's godmother (*compah* for godfather) which elevated that person above others and into the realm of being a physical guarding angel. Often, the title was extended. Nonna had friends from her home town of Rapino, Italy, with whom she was very close. Among her friends were five sisters. When she was young, she christened a daughter of one of the sisters, and suddenly all five sisters became *commahs,* and their husbands, *compahs.* All of Nonna's children extended the title to the five sisters. I was called *compahucci,* little God child. Again this was all done out of respect and to show honor.

Sometimes if no spiritual connection was afforded, two women would exchange flowers or a gift and declare each other *commare di fiore,* godmothers of flower. With this exchange came the promise of prayers for each other. Again, it was a title of respect that made someone special in your life. Heaven forbid if you, out of stupidity or laziness, forget to call someone by their title of respect, for if you did forget you were immediately reprimanded and humiliated. Disrespect was never tolerated in an Italian family.

Now, let me explain something else to you: You have not lived a viewing unless you have been to an Italian viewing. All Italian-American viewings during this time were held in the homes of the deceased. To go to a funeral parlor was unthinkable and a great insult to the deceased. It was a sign of disrespect by the family. So in the comfort of the home, viewings took on the character of being very private and in a free atmosphere, and in this atmosphere things happened that were never thought of or could be imagined. To begin with, the entire family was expected to wear black. This included distant, distant relatives as well as immediate family. Black was everywhere: black dresses, stockings, shawls, veils, suits, ties, arm bands, and shoes, even the white handkerchiefs the women mourners used to wipe their many, many tears were trimmed with a black border or black lace.

There were cries, screams, and pathetic wails. There were fainting bodies, pulling of hair and clothes, stamping of feet, falling on corpses, and grabbing of corpses. Many times the men stood stoically nearby ready to catch the fainters, restrain the climbers, and control the hysterics.

Every person who went to the casket to view the body was told something about the deceased by a member of the family, and the deceased in turn was told who was approaching their casket just in case they did not know who was there. Above all, it was expected of the family to honor and respect the dead with a long period of mourning that often lasted for years, sometimes for decades. Immediately after death, members of the immediate family were forbidden to go to places of enjoyment such as movies, operas, theaters, and, God forbid, dances. The radio was not permitted to be played and no one was allowed to whistle, hum, or sing in the house at least for a month after the burial.

I remember a viewing of a distant cousin of Nonna. The family was big. The body was at rest in the living room, and the family, relatives, friends, and neighbors were in the kitchen. A meal was being cooked on the gas range. All four jets were working. In the oven, bread and cookies were baking. Zio Orazio, the deceased, had four daughters and each of them seemed to be attending one of the pots on the gas range, while the many grandchildren were serving visiting relatives, family, and friends. Zia Maria, the widow, sat in a prominent seat and many people were around her. There was talk and funny stories, situations, and sayings being shared, and everyone was laughing and enjoying themselves. Suddenly the front door of the house opened and a friend of the family came in. The daughters left their pots and Zia Maria was helped into the living room to greet the visitor. There were cries and laments; there were words of pain and sadness. This went on for some time when suddenly, Zia Filamena, a distant relative, declared "*abbastanza*," enough. Zia Marie grabbed the hand of the last arrival and escorted her and her husband into the kitchen. "*Vene! Sede! Manga!*" Come! Sit! Eat! she ordered and soon the kitchen was back to cooking, talking, remembering, and laughing.

All these things were expected if the deceased was loved. If these things did not happen and were missing, then there was something wrong with the family's love or there was something bad, shameful, or sinful about the deceased.

Nothing I am saying is in disrespect or mockery because death to all Italians was a time to celebrate life, the memory of their existence, and our belief in a life hereafter with the promise of eternal love and happiness. Italians are emotional people. Their music, art, and literature show this, and they often celebrate happiness and sadness with the same emotions and tears. The lamenting and carrying on was part of the emotions and passion of the Italians. Everyone understood all the tears, cries, and screams because the living are in pain from the loss of companionship and not for the deceased, who we all knew was in a better place.

I understood all these things, as did my cousins and all my family, but this viewing of the little baby somehow bothered me. The sight of a small white casket and a little baby in it stirred up a lot of questions about the unfairness of the death of innocents and why God would permit such a thing to happen. As a result, I was very quiet and pensive all the way home from Commah Seppina's house.

As always, Nonna knew something was wrong. Later that day as I picked up one of my school books to study, Nonna came over to me and leaned over my shoulder. I knew she had no idea what I was writing because she could not read cursive English that well, so I suspected something was on her mind.

She asked, "So, what is my genius grandson learning today?"

"Nothing," I said.

"All that is nothing?" she asked, roughly pointing to the books before me.

She stood erect and for no reason other than out of habit, she began wiping her hands on her apron.

"It looks like a lot of something to be nothing, Vinzee."

"Sorry. I'm doing my Geography homework. Sister Mary Immaculata wants us to write the capitals of all the countries in South America."

"And then what do you have to do?"

"Study them for a test and then I'm finished."

"Good," she said quickly, turned, and walked away. "Then we will have coffee and some of my *biscotti*"—Italian biscuit.

I smiled with approval and scribbled the capitals from Argentina to Venezuela in seconds, promising myself that I would study them later. Finished, I threw my pencil in my school bag, slammed my Geography and copy books shut, and threw them also in my bag. Quickly I buckled up my bag and tossed it on one of the dining room chairs.

The smell of coffee was all around me, so I immediately raced to the back kitchen. When I arrived, I instantly felt warmth and love embrace me.

All the cups, spoons, napkins, cookies, Karo, and milk were in place; even the coffee had been poured.

I threw myself on a chair just as Nonna began stirring her coffee, and I heard the familiar click-clack-click-clack rhythm of her spoon hitting and sliding around the inside of her cup.

I quickly fixed my coffee, anxious to savor the rich taste of my favorite beverage, and just as I was about to take my first sip, Nonna remarked, "You looked very bothered today after the viewing. I know you are used to going to viewings, as it is something that God has asked us to do, 'Blessed are they that mourn…,' so I don't think that was what was bothering you, for your family and the good Sisters taught you better."

I put my cup down and looked at her. I was always amazed how she could read my thoughts and my feelings so freely. This happened so many times that I was certain she, like so many other Nonnas, had some special powers. It was a special gift from God reserved only for grandmothers, and my Nonna had cornered the market on this gift.

"It was the little white casket and the little baby in it that bothered me."

"And why? Don't you think babies have to die?"

For one quick moment I was shocked with her words. They seemed so cold and harsh and I wondered, *How could she say that?*

I quickly remembered that I was listening to a mother who had lost one of her own—her oldest child. My Aunt Giovannina had died when she was four years old, so Nonna had experienced the loss of a baby.

I began to put myself in reverse and silently toned down my shock at her coldness.

"I can't understand why God would do such a bad thing." My statement was addressed to her and her loss, and not the loss of the baby I viewed earlier that day.

"Because God needs innocent people in heaven, to be shadows of angels," she said simply. She looked at me hoping she had satisfied the bad taste I had, but when she saw she had not satisfied me, she said, "A little story by a great Italian saint."

I immediately took a sip of my coffee and the entire world was becoming right again, for there was Nonna, the back kitchen, coffee, me, and a story.

"Many years ago, heaven was occupied by archangels. Did you know that? Well, it is true. There were only a few of them: Michael, Gabriel, and Raphael. These archangels were the defenders, messengers, and healers of the world, and they did these great things because of the will of God, and because God needed these things to be done for Him.

"The other groups of angels were the guardian angels, and they were always so busy trying to keep people out of trouble by whispering in their ears what was good and directing them to do the right thing. This was such an important and big job that they could do nothing else. They seldom came back to heaven unless they had to get their wings fixed after a difficult battle with a bad angel, or to get instructions on how to help their responsibility, or give reports on the person they were guarding, or to take a soul back to God for judgment.

"All the other angels that roamed around the heavens were still young. They were cherubs. They were young, fat, and rosy cheeked and always playing around heaven. Of course they did have to do some work, like fix and polish the stars, move and fluff the clouds, make thunder by moving the furniture around in heaven, and even play catch with lightning bolts. When God wanted rain, they would wring the clouds, and if God wanted snow, they would jump up and down on the clouds to loosen the snowflakes. They also had the big job of gathering all the colors in the world to paint rainbows after storms. Because these cherubs were so small, it took a lot of them to do this work. When they had to push the breeze around the world, hundreds of them had to blow together, and if it was a wind, it took thousands of them. To create an earthquake, it took hundreds of thousands of them jumping up and down on the earth just to make a small tremble. Besides all these things to do, they also had the all-important job of filling the heavens with songs of praises to God day and night.

"Now one day God took a long look at the earth and saw that a lot of people were being born, and He was running out of guardian angels. There was no way to promote the cherubs, because it took so many of them to do the work He had assigned them.

"So while God was in heaven working on this problem, the devil was busy working on King Herod. The Wise Men had left King Herod so afraid of the 'King of Israel' that Herod had all the young, fat, rosy-cheeked babies killed, hoping to kill the Baby Jesus. Because these babies were as innocent as the cherubs and because they looked like cherubs when they arrived in heaven, God quickly made them take over the older cherubs' jobs and He promoted the older cherubs to being guardian angels for newborn babies."

She returned to stirring her coffee and the loud clink-clank, clink-clank became the only sound in the room.

"So whenever God needs cherubs, he calls one of the babies back home to heaven?" I asked, still thinking this was a cruel thing for a God of love and mercy to do.

"Ah, now here is where being grown-up is important." She was smiling. "Remember the story of the Holy Innocents? King Herod listened to the devil. Who do you think got blamed for the Holy Innocents? God. The devil knows that taking babies always gets mommies and daddies mad at God. So the devil helps babies get sick and die to make God look bad. The devil sometimes doesn't win because many times God cures the sick baby and the baby lives. God does that when he has enough cherubs in heaven, but when God needs more cherubs, He will take the baby. What you have to understand, Vinzee, is God accepts the babies with more love than the love mommies and daddies have for them. In fact, many saints tell us that God loves more than any of us can understand.

"The babies will grow up to do some of the work of guardian angels. These babies will sing and praise God and always be busy. They are happy because they are with God, and they are constantly doing His will. Always remember, Vinzee, God does not destroy, He only creates. He helps mothers and fathers create, and He helps parents continue to create their babies until the babies become grown-ups."

She stopped stirring her coffee.

"Understand?"

"In a way," I said, knowing that I had to digest this story further.

After coffee, I washed our cups, and Nonna started cleaning the house and finally started to cook.

I returned to my Geography book and started studying the capitals of the South American countries.

Without looking or without asking, I knew what kind of meal Nonna was making. Every Monday was soup day. She was going to make homemade chicken or beef soup and French toast to go with the soup. She would also be frying chicken and potatoes or making mashed potatoes. I knew this because every Italian knew by the day of the week what they would have for dinner. Tuesdays were always *macaroni*— store-bought macaroni. Wednesday was American food— corn, potatoes, green vegetables, and fried fish. During the War, President Roosevelt asked all Americans not to eat meat on Wednesdays to help with the rations for the servicemen, and being a Catholic at that time meant an added day of no meat. Thursdays were *macaroni* and again store bought, but not *spaghetti*. Friday was always fish day, because Catholics were not permitted to each meat on Fridays. There were always the alternatives of *pasta fagioli*—pasta and beans, *pasta ceci*—pasta and chick peas, lentil soup, or my favorite *macaroni olio e agilo*—macaroni with garlic and olive oil. Saturdays were anything days. Normally it was whatever was left over from the other meals or just sandwiches. Sometimes, if we had the ration stamps for flour, we would have pizza. Every Sunday was homemade spaghetti with meatballs and *braccioli* in tomato gravy.

This may sound like we ate the same things each week—well, we did—but the difference was Nonna's cooking. There was always a twist to her cooking. If she was making gravy [sauce], she would make heavy, light, or marinated gravy. She would make an omelet out of nothing, season it with anything, and you would have the best of everything. Nothing was ever wasted in her kitchen. She cooked everything and disguised it so well that it didn't matter what it was before, because it tasted great at dinner.

Some of the seasonings she added to her cooking were not found in jars or bottles, for she would season her food with heavy amounts of love, care, pride, joy, tradition, and many other thoughtful things.

As Nonna always said, "It is the same, yet it is with different love. What we eat is a bigger menu than what Jesus, Mary, and Joseph had so we must always be thankful to God, because He gives us bigger and better menus."

After I finished my studying, I went out and played for an hour, then returned home just before my cousins came home from school and before my mother and aunts came home from work. I went into the kitchen and found Nonna still preparing dinner for the family. I was a little uncomfortable with our earlier conversation. Something was still bothering me. I didn't know what it was, but something definitely was missing.

The minute I walked into the back kitchen, Nonna glanced over her shoulder at me and said nothing, but again, she sensed something was wrong.

"So, you came back because you are not satisfied with my story."

She sighed loudly.

I don't know if this sigh was from frustration with me or annoyance at my bothering her or just plain disgust.

Without any further hesitation, she started, "Vinzee, you must remember life is not white or black—it is gray. Life has a little bit of happiness and a little bit of sadness; it has a little bit of goodness and a little bit of badness, so it is gray. The bad and sad thing you saw was the little body of a baby, but look what God does with such a bad and sad thing. Because He never creates bad things, He makes good things out of the bad which we or the devil made. When an older person dies, they go to God with many things in their minds and memories. Death is a sad thing for them because they did not want to leave life; they had lived it and tasted the sweetness of it. When a baby dies, they go to God with only love. They don't carry shopping bags or suitcases with them. They are not afraid of death, and they go from love to a greater Love and from care to a greater Care. They have so much of this Love and Care that they share it and let some of it drop to earth. Sometimes babies become as guardian angels to their parents or even to their brothers and sisters or their whole family. The people who suffer the most with the death of a baby are those who have to live on, but never does the baby suffer."

She stopped cooking and walked to the sink to rinse off the lettuce for our salad.

After a few moments she continued, "Each life, no matter how quick it passes through the world, leaves a mark on the world. God knows this, for we are His creation. He is Good and from Good comes good. What is left for us to do is to find the good in the life that passed by us."

She stopped rinsing and looked up at the wall above the sink.

"I had my baby for a short time. It was a good time, but when she left me to become as a cherub and to help God with His creation instead of helping me, it was a bitter time. I had given something back to God, and God did not forget me, for He gave me my own special cherub. Did it hurt? Of course, but I will always be my Giovannina's *Momma.* In life and death, I will always be that. When my baby died, I remember thinking this is the way the mothers of the Holy Innocents felt; this is the way Mary hurt. Those mothers and Mary also had cried and also had felt pain. I remember thinking about what happened as a result of these bad times. The mothers saved Jesus from Herod, and Mary became the Queen of Heaven with all those cherubs and us as her children. When I die, I will help Mary with her cherubs, because she knows I was like her—a mother who hurt."

I walked quietly out of the back kitchen knowing that tears were in Nonna's eyes, but they were tears of joy, for on the other side she would always be what she was on this side—a mother.

◆ YOU MIGHT HAVE MISSED SOMETHING ◆

One day, without thinking, I remarked to Nonna that I could not understand why people went to the cemetery to visit graves. After all, "There wasn't anything there except dirt."

She reacted quietly and said with soft conviction, "You have to go back. You might have missed something. You may have to recall a mistake that needs correction. Besides, when we visit graves we bring back memories, and memories always make the dead come to life again."

I didn't understand. I remained silent, running her words through my mind trying to make sense of what she said.

She detected that my silence meant I was confused, so she continued, "There was a great writer who once told a story about something like this…let me see if I can remember."

As she thought about her story, she finished cleaning the gas range with her towel and walked to the kitchen sink to rinse the cloth in hot sudsy water. She then walked to the porcelain table with the towel and a bar of Fels-Naphtha soap. After she scrubbed the table and gave the kitchen chairs a few quick swipes, she said, "Oh yes, now I remember. Come, sit down. Let's have some coffee."

Nonna got the coffee pot off the gas range and stood by the kitchen table waiting, as I quickly raced around the kitchen getting paper napkins, brown sugar, cups, and spoons from the metal cabinet and the milk from the ice box. When all was set in place, she poured the coffee and before sitting down, she folded two paper napkins and placed them next to our cups. She sat down. With both hands, she picked up her cup of hot coffee and took a long refreshing sip. She wet her lips, folded her arms and rested them on the table, and leaning forward slightly, she began the story.

"After Jesus was arrested, all the Apostles, fearing for their lives, ran away. Of course, we know that Peter and John followed Jesus, but the others just ran away. Later, some of them did become brave, and hiding themselves in the great crowd, watched as Jesus carried His Cross through the small and narrow streets of Jerusalem. Some of them even made it up to the top of Golgotha and there they hid behind some big trees or large boulders. From these hiding places, they watched Jesus. Of course, Jesus knew they were there because no one can hide from the eyes of God, no one, especially those who have done wrong.

"Within hours after Jesus' death and burial, the Apostles slowly began to gather. They needed to get together because they were lost without Jesus, and now they only had each other. One by one, bewildered, afraid, and sad, they returned to the room where they had celebrated the Last Supper. This room was their usual meeting place; it was the home of Saint Mark's parents. When finally they all settled down, they began talking and comparing news, feelings, fears, and thoughts. It was during these talks that they learned of Judas' death, Peter's denials, and young John's courage to stay with Jesus until the bitter end. They listened to John's account of all that happened on Golgotha, and some of them wept openly as John spoke of the horrible death Jesus endured.

"Finally, they began to tell their own stories, which were filled with cowardliness and fear, and most importantly, regrets and sadness. When they had finished telling what they had failed to do, they began to grow silent and still.

"You see, Vinzee, each of them began to feel the weight of their shame," Nonna said, taking another sip of coffee and breaking the story. She softly wiped her lips with the paper napkin and neatly folded it next to her cup. Wetting her lips again, she continued, "The rest of that night and the next day, they sat silently in small groups or alone. Their shame was so great that they could not look at each other. Many of them cried in secret and asked Jesus for forgiveness. As suppertime drew near, the Holy Women discovered they needed some provisions, so some of the Apostles volunteered to go out after sunset and get the food they needed. So one by one, those who had offered to go slipped out of the house and into the early night to obtain whatever was needed for their supper. Truthfully, those who volunteered wanted to be alone. They needed to think without the accusing eyes of the other Apostles. Being away from the others, they knew they would be able to think truthfully about their failure and feel their own shame and not the shame of each other. What they did not know was that God wanted them to be alone, because being alone would help them find themselves.

"Matthew was one of those who volunteered and he was told to get some bread. As he walked, he found himself remembering the time he was a better Apostle. So he went to the place in Jerusalem where he first saw Jesus. When he arrived at that same place, he remembered how excited he became when he first heard Jesus' voice, which was some time before Jesus called him. He stood crying, wanting once more to hear the sound of Jesus' voice calling his name and the demand of 'Come, follow Me.'

"Another volunteer was Jude Thaddeus who went out to find some fish. After he bought the fish, he walked to the place where he once played with Jesus as a child when their families came to Jerusalem for the Holy Days. He wanted to remember the innocent years he had with Jesus, when things were simple and filled with love.

"Much later, Philip, Simon the Zealot, and Bartholomew went out to obtain some wine, figs, dates, and fruit. As they walked, Simon said that he needed to go to Golgotha, because he felt this was the place he had been the most cowardly. He was one of those who had hidden behind a big boulder.

"'I followed the death procession to the Mount,' Simon the Zealot told Philip and Bartholomew, 'but did not stay for the Crucifixion. I was afraid of being recognized by someone. I need to go back to that place and ask forgiveness,' he concluded sadly.

"Philip admitted to a similar story, but added, 'I did not get to Golgotha. I was hiding in the crowd, but when I saw some of the Temple guards, who I knew, I ran away before they saw me. I think I need to walk the way Jesus walked.' He excused himself and disappeared down one of the small dark streets.

"Bartholomew listened to his two companions but said nothing. He seemed to be at a loss as to where he had been the most cowardly, so he simply walked with Simon the Zealot out the City Gate.

"As these two Apostles walked, they each went into their own thoughts and into their own sufferings. As they continued toward the Mount, Bartholomew purposely slowed down, fell behind Simon, and eventually lost sight of him. He walked aimlessly with no idea where he was to go. He just walked deep in his own thoughts of Jesus, feeling heavy with disgrace. Eventually, to his surprise, he found himself standing just outside the gate to the Garden of Gethsemane.

"*Oh yes,* he thought, *this is where I had to come. This was the place of my greatest weakness. The place I was the most cowardly.*

"He cautiously walked into the Garden, and slowly made his way to that part of the Garden he remembered being in when Jesus was arrested. When he felt he had found the very

same place he had rested that night, he sat there and immediately grew uneasy, but did not know why.

"In a little while, he began to remember that long ago
night. It had been a night free of problems; it had been a
night of happiness and joy. It was a night of celebration and
they had celebrated hard, took much wine, and ate much
food. They went to the Garden to pray, but only Jesus prayed.
Sadly, unwillingly, he went further back to that night, and his
remembering began to grow heavy. He remembered being
stirred from his heavy sleep by the sounds of distant footsteps
and loud mumbling. He instantaneously knew it was trouble
but didn't know what kind of trouble. For some unknown
reason, he remembered knowing those approaching were the
Temple Guards and they were looking for Jesus. He kept his
eyes closed hoping that the sounds and his suspicions would
go away. He knew he should call Jesus to try to help Him
escape, but he was too afraid to move. He thought of waking
the others from their sleep, knowing that together they could
help Jesus, but his fear had more strength over him than his
good sense. He thought of escaping, but he had no courage
to move.

"He remembered all these things as if they were happening for the first time. His fear, his sleepiness, his lack
of courage, and his decision to do nothing to help Jesus
weighed him down with disgrace. So he again did what he
had done that night, he covered himself with his cloak, hid
deep in his hood, and pushed himself further into the bushes
behind him. He allowed everything to happen, again. As he
remembered doing these vile things, his very flesh began to
ache with dishonor and shame. He began to grow so sad that
warm tears slipped from his eyes and down his cheeks. His
mouth grew dry and his heart beat rapidly. In defense against
his re-lived fears, he pushed and hid himself further into the
bushes, into their darkness.

"He then heard a sound and it quickly drew him back to the present time. With terror, he turned his head in the direction of the sound. Through his half-closed eyes and shadowed face, he saw a man working around the Garden.

"The man was bending over picking up twigs and leaves and sometimes stopping to water the flowers and plants from a jar he was carrying. The man abruptly stopped working and stood upright. He looked over to where Bartholomew was hiding. With no hesitation, the man walked quickly to the hidden Apostle.

"'Please, sir,' he said softly. 'Please come out. I shall not harm you.'

"Bartholomew pretended he did not hear the man. Again the man asked Bartholomew to stop hiding. Reluctantly, Bartholomew came out of the dark bushes. He brushed himself clean and looked at the man very carefully. Unexpectedly, he recognized this man, and a new fear swelled within himself.

"'Do I know you?' the Gardener asked, as he looked more closely at Bartholomew's shadowed and partly hidden face.

"'No!' Bartholomew replied quickly. 'I am a stranger in this place,' and turning sharply, he began to walk away. He wanted to—he *had* to—escape the man and the Garden.

"'Oh, please stay a while. Isn't this a beautiful Garden? You know, for years I walked by this place and never stopped to look at it. Now I tend it every day and I believe it is the most perfect, most beautiful place in all creation. Don't you agree?'

"'Yes,' Bartholomew quickly answered as he raised his hand to tug at his hood, wanting to obscure his face from the brightness of the full moon. He didn't want to look at the man, nor did he want to be recognized by him. The idea of being this close to the man made Bartholomew tremble with total fear.

"'Come. Walk with me, please,' the Gardener pleaded as he turned to walk along one of the small winding paths of the Garden.

"Bartholomew reluctantly joined him. Together they casually walked silently past the olive trees and the many bushes and shrubs that grew in the Garden.

"'This place is so beautiful that I have vowed to remain here forever. I have promised to tend to its beauty till I die.'

"'You were here the night Jesus was arrested?' Bartholomew heard himself ask. The words he heard were not from his own mouth or from his own thoughts, for he would not have asked such a question, for to do so would draw too much attention to him. But yet, he heard the words. He had betrayed himself and this made his heart beat quickly. His chest ached from the heavy throb of his heart and his ears pounded with each heartbeat. He needed to breathe, but was afraid even to take a breath of air.

"'Yes!' the Gardener replied with ease. 'It was a beautiful night. Tell me, were you here?'

"Bartholomew recoiled under the question.

"'I must go,' he said as he wrapped his cloak around himself and walked quickly away.

"'Please, sir, come back anytime you wish, for I shall be here tending this place until God wills that I leave. You are welcome here anytime.'

"Bartholomew's walk soon turned into a run. As he exited the Garden, he glanced back and saw the Gardener again tending the Garden. He raced back to the Upper Room, and when he finally reached Mark's home, he soon felt at peace, safe and secure. As bad as the experience was, he was certain that it was meant for him to go back to the Garden. If he had not gone back this night, then it would have been another night, for eventually he had to remember what he wanted to forget. He had to face what he had not done and what he had made happen there, and above all he had to ask forgiveness.

"You see, Vinzee," Nonna said with sad resolve, "Bartholomew was like Matthew, Simon, Philip, and Thaddeus. They all had to face, recall what they had not done for Jesus. Just like we have to remember what we forgot to do for those who we loved in our lives who have gone to God. Those who are gone are still part of us. They are always part of our lives, for they touched, walked, ate, sang, and danced with us just like Jesus was part of the Apostles."

She again stopped talking and raised her cup to her lips. She took two quick sips, and then a third long sip of the coffee, finally returning her cup to its saucer.

"Months later when the Apostles were more sure of themselves, because the Holy Ghost had filled them with the desire to tell the whole world the story of Jesus, the Twelve sat in council and discussed what missionary work they would do. Each was given a country in which to preach the word of Jesus. The Apostle James, who everyone called the 'Less' because he was so short in height, was assigned Jerusalem and all the places that had been made holy by Jesus' presence.

"Just before Bartholomew left for his mission to Armenia and India, he took James the Less aside and told him that he should not worry about tending the Garden of Gethsemane, because of the Gardener who was taking care of it. After telling James this, Bartholomew and the others left and James remained in Jerusalem.

"Sometime later, James went to the Garden to see the Gardener whom Bartholomew had spoken about. When James saw who the man was, James simply blessed him and left the Garden, knowing that the man had been blessed more than any one he knew. James never returned again, for he knew the Garden was in good hands.

"Many months after this, the enemies of Jesus learned that the Christians were using sites which Jesus often frequented as meeting places. So, they went to the Garden of Gethsemane with the hopes of destroying it, but when they were met by the Gardener, whom they recognized as being one of them, they decided to forget about doing any harm to the Garden, for they were sure none of the Christians would go there."

Nonna got up from her chair and gathered our cups and spoons. She walked slowly to the sink and began washing our dishes in sudsy water. As she washed, she continued, "So you see, Vinzee, you must always go back. We learn from the things and the people in our past. Going back is a gift from God. He created in us the ability to return to our yesterdays and relive our faults and goodness. When Matthew, Mark, Luke, and John went back in their memories, God made them write the Gospels. When we read the Bible, we go back and remember all that God did for us and all He wants us to do for Him. Going back helps us correct our mistakes and make amends. Matthew had to go back, to be called again. Thaddeus had to become a child again. Simon and Philip had to finish what they had left unfinished. Bartholomew had to face his lack of courage, and James had to face the Gardener who had been blessed even more than any of the Apostles."

She picked up the *mapeen,* the dish towel, and started drying some of the dishes she had just washed. She turned to me and continued, "Saint Mary Magdalene, Joann, and the other Holy Women went back to Jesus' tomb because they felt they had not done a good job preparing Jesus for burial. We go to the cemetery just to make sure we haven't forgotten to do or say something to the dead. We also go back to make certain we didn't forgot to get something from them. Being dead only stops us from seeing people, not learning from them or understanding things better. Always go back; you might have forgotten something."

With a fling of her hand, she commanded, "Now, go out and play, and remember what you have learned."

I did as she ordered but could not concentrate on playing ball. Something was left unsaid and finally the unsaid bothered me so much that I raced home to Nonna's side as fast as I could.

"Nonna, whatever happened to the Gardener?"

"Oh, he died a martyr's death. After James the Less was martyred, the enemies of Jesus began to search out all the Christians. They found out that the Gardener had been a follower of Jesus, so they stabbed him to death."

"What was this saint's name? I would like to pray to him."

"Well, Mister Wise Guy, I am surprised. I thought you would have figured it all out by now."

She smiled, wet her lips, looked at me and said, "His name was Malchus."

Still seeing me confused, she chuckled. "Still no? Well, he was the man who lost his ear to Peter's sword and the man on whom Jesus performed His last miracle."

You see, always go back. You might have missed something.

◆ IN THAT STABLE LONG AGO ◆

This is one of Nonna's greatest stories and one that I love the most. I do not remember why she told me this story, but I do remember she told it every Christmas and each time she told it her details became more creative and clearer.

I recall this story each Christmas, but I seldom tell it because it seemed to be something personal. I hope you enjoy this tale and that it finds its way into your heart and your family's heart, as it did mine.

It was a cold winter's night. It was one of those winter nights that had no wind, so the cold stayed and stood around you.

The sky was empty of clouds. There was nothing in the thick, dark-blue sky but a bright, shining full moon that made the countryside blue and steel gray. The moonlight fell onto the earth and made big, long, dark shadows. There were thousands of blinking stars that seemed to be playing and dancing in the heavens.

In the side of a hill in a shallow cave that was used as a stable, three animals stood silent and still. Occasionally they would look out over the weather-beaten wooden fence and into the night. They were tired, but not from the day's work, for they were too old to work and had not worked in many, many months. They were tired from being nothing and doing nothing. They were the leftovers of a stable that at one time was filled with cows, hens, roosters, oxen, donkeys, and sheep, but these were hard times and the Roman taxes had stripped their owner of all these productive animals. The three animals left were called Hava the Cow, Ova the Hen, and Shalev the Ox.

"You animals will stay with me," their owner had said many months ago, "until Rome finds they can use the useless."

So they stayed, waiting, but Rome's hand never reached them. Now old, unproductive, tired, and sagging—unable to milk, lay eggs, or toil—they were far too useless for anything but slaughter. As they waited in the stable, the three of them became thick and strong friends.

"It's a quiet night, do not you think?" Hava the Cow said, as she slowly pushed the hay in the stall into the corner with the idea of making a comfortable bed for the night.

"Yes, you know I was thinking the same thing just this moment. It seems as if night and everything is waiting for something to happen," Ova the Hen said, as she looked out into the night from between the wooden slats of the fence.

"Yeah, it does seem to be a very strange night," Hava continued. "You know, when things are this quiet, it usually means bad weather is coming."

"I hope not," blurted Shalev the Ox in his deep baritone voice, "my poor ol' bones cannot take damp cold or rainy weather anymore."

"I understand what you are saying, but still, this is a strange night and I feel something unusual is going to happen, maybe even very soon," Hava insisted with an all-knowing voice.

"Well, if it is bad weather coming, we should move further into the cave and away from whatever is coming our way," Shalev remarked, as he began to lumber to the back of the stable and to the back of the cave.

"Shalev is right, we should seek better shelter," Ova said, as she scurried away from the fence and quickly passed the Ox's massive body.

Hava slowly turned to join them when suddenly she saw something coming up the road to the stable.

It was a human!

"A human is coming," Hava mooed, and the others quickly turned to see what she was seeing.

Sure enough, coming up the road of the small hill toward the stable was a young, handsome man with a dark black beard. Protecting himself from the cold, he tightly wrapped his cloak about him, as he gently and patiently led with a rope a tired and old limping donkey.

"Hurry, Eliyah, I must get back to Miriam," the young man said softly with much concern and love in his voice.

The donkey moved a little faster, and when they reached the fence, the young man tied the rope around the post of the fence and swiftly turned and walked briskly away and down the road.

Hava, Ova, and Shalev walked slowly to the visitor by the fence.

"Good evening, I am Shalev," the Ox said with an air of leadership in his voice, "and these are my stable friends, Hava and Ova. So now, who are you?"

"His name is Eliyah," Hava responded with impatience, for she disliked Shalev when he tried to act like the protector of the sable.

"Where are you from?" she asked tenderly as she turned her attention to the donkey.

"From Nazareth. My master and mistress are here for the Roman census," Eliyah replied as he turned his head to look down the road.

"That is quite a distance to have traveled; you must be tired and sore."

"A little," the donkey said as he continued to look down the road.

"That limp must have bothered you a great deal."

"My limp! Oh, I forgot all about it. It does not hurt me. Am I still limping?"

The three stable friends looked at each other in disbelief and returned their attention to the donkey, who continued to look down the hill and road he had just climbed.

"We saw your master, but where is your mistress?" Ova questioned.

Eliyah turned, and looking at the stable animals, answered, "Oh, she is standing by the door of the inn getting warmed up. The innkeeper told her she could warm up a bit before coming here to rest the night."

"She is coming here?" Shalev bellowed.

"Yes. There is no room at the inn and they have no place to go, but here."

"Oh good, human company, what a pleasant surprise!" Ova said.

Eliyah turned and again looked down the road.

"Where are these people going to stay?" Shalev objected.

"In the space we do not occupy!" Ova retorted quickly.

"Sure, that is easy for you to say. You do not take up that much space, but I am big and I need space," Shalev bragged.

"You also have a big mouth," Hava interjected as she continued to stare at Eliyah the donkey. "So be quiet. It seems our donkey friend is worried about something. Why do you keep looking down the road, Eliyah?"

The question drew Eliyah's attention, so he turned and observed the expectant look on the faces of the three animals.

"I am concerned about my mistress. She is with child, and though I am not an expert on these things, I am sure her time is near."

"Did you hear that, Ova? A mother is coming to be with us."

"Oh, Hava, it has been so long. We must make things ready."

"Not I," shouted Shalev. "I still do not think we have the room, and with a child, we will have less room."

"Oh, Shalev, stop being such a bully and a bigger fool. We always help humans. It is our command, so be still and stop worrying about yourself and be good enough to think of others," Hava said roughly. Her patience with Shalev was always short.

"What are your owners like?" Ova asked.

"They are financially poor, but they are rich in other ways. There is a softness about them. They speak softly and gently, not only to each other, but to everyone they meet. When they speak to each other, they speak with more than just love. It seems they have a reverence for each other," Eliyah said, and again turned his eyes to the road.

"Oh, they sound so caring, so kindly," Ova stated with overwhelming emotions.

"They cannot be that nice. Look how they made him, a lame donkey, walk all that distance and most likely carried the woman, the mother to be, on his back," Shalev smirked.

Again, Eliyah turned his sight to the stable dwellers. "But my leg never hurt me, and my mistress, Miriam, was not heavy. I know you may find this strange and maybe you may not believe me, but before Yosef bought me from my owner, I was unable to stand on this leg without being in great pain, and because they did not have the money to buy a better or healthier donkey, they had to take me. When I heard they were coming to Bethlehem, I believed them insane. I knew I would not be able to make the journey, yet they prepared for the trip, seeming to believe that I would be of use to them and be able to travel that great distance."

Silently, the three stable animals stood listening. They were no authorities, but they knew when they were in the presence of something unusual or astounding.

Eliyah lowered his back legs and sat on the cold hardened earth.

"With their small provisions and my mistress on my back, and walking all those miles, all that distance, my leg never hurt. The pain is gone and I am sure it will never return, even though I walk with a limp. I do not know how my leg is painless, because I am only a stupid donkey, but I believe it will remain painless because I belong to Miriam and Yosef."

"Oh, I just cannot wait to be with your two owners. I am so anxious to see if they are really like you say and to see what other wonders surround them," Ova stated with great excitement.

"Shh," Hava whispered. "I think I hear someone coming."

Eliyah sprung to all four legs, and with the other animals, looked in the direction of the road. In the distance they saw the young-bearded, handsome Yosef, slowly walking up the small hill supporting the young, beautiful, and delicate maiden, Miriam.

"Oh my, her time is near," Hava whispered. "Oh, Ova, we will be needed tonight."

Eliyah walked quickly to the young couple. His silent, but rapid approach, made the young couple realize he was offering his assistance. Yosef carefully lifted Miriam on the donkey's back, and the donkey began walking slowly and carefully to the stable. As he walked, it seemed as if his feet were barely touching the cold, hard ground beneath his hooves.

The animals in the stable stepped back and away, to allow their human visitors as much room as possible.

Yosef opened the gate to the stable and gently guided Eliyah through it. Yosef removed his cloak, exposing himself to the cold night air. He threw the cloak on the hay nearby, and then cautiously he helped Miriam off Eliyah's back.

"Are you all right, Miriam?" the young husband asked, and all the animals sensed his deep concern and love for the young maiden.

"Yes, Yosef, I am fine, just a bit tired," Miriam responded, and the animals felt her gentleness and her loving care.

"Here, rest on my cloak."

"Oh, Yosef, you cannot give me your cloak. It is much too cold to be without one."

"I am fine. I will find some wood and build a fire for warmth, and all will be good."

"There is no wood," Shalev said in a low voice to the other animals that stood engrossed by the young couple. "The shepherds took all the twigs and branches this afternoon because they were certain it would be cold on their watch tonight."

"What shall they do?" Eliyah asked. "It is too cold for my mistress. Without a fire, they will die of cold."

"Ova, look at Miriam's face. She knows her time is close. She must be in pain." Hava said.

"Oh, how will they warm the Babe, Hava? We must do something. Please think of something!" Ova said in a choked voice.

"Miriam, if I leave, will you be all right?" Yosef asked. "I will go back and get our other provisions and blankets, which I left behind at the bottom of the road. While there, I will look for firewood. I will be back. If you need me, call."

Yosef hurried through the gate of the stable and disappeared down the road.

Miriam let out a heavy sigh and her face relaxed.

"Oh, Yahweh, let this be Your time and let all be well," the animals heard the young maiden say.

"It's going to happen," Hava said in a low hushed tone.

Miriam's sigh turned into a smothered prayer.

"Now…." A bright blinding light that came from Miriam overpowered Hava's word and it brought daylight to the night.

The four animals turned their heads away, needing to protect their eyes from the blinding light. They could actually feel the light; it seemed to press against them and stayed around and over them for several heavy and intense moments.

Suddenly they heard the cry of a Babe. Turning, they found Miriam holding a Child, which she wrapped in Yosef's cloak.

"A Baby!" Shalev said in a hushed tone.

"Yes, a Baby Boy," Hava gasped.

"What are we going to do?" Ova asked.

"What can we do?" Eliyah replied.

"Listen…," Hava said.

"What?"

"Birds…I hear birds singing! And I hear the sounds of other animals. Do you hear it also?"

"Yes. Yes," Ova answered excitedly. "The night is alive with our families."

All of a sudden, the birds began coming to the front of the stable dropping twigs and small branches of trees.

"They are gathering wood to warm the Babe," Eliyah said.

"They will need much more wood. Those small twigs will never warm a baby," Shalev said, and he walked quickly to the fence of the stable and with all his might, pushed against the fence, knocking loose several wooden boards and slats.

"There, that should help," he said with a smile and a great deal of pride in his voice.

"Why, Shalev, you are so strong and so smart," Hava said, pleased that her old friend had shown he cared.

When they looked up, Yosef was standing at the front of the stable. He quickly fell to his knees and in a low voice began to praise God. Slowly, carefully, reverently, he reached over and touched the head of the Baby.

"Are you well, Miriam?" he asked without taking his eyes off the Babe.

"Yes, Yosef, but we must hurry and clean the Baby and wrap him with the swaddling clothes my mother, Hannah, gave me."

Yosef quickly began unraveling and unpacking the provisions he had fetched, and Miriam went about cleaning and wrapping the Babe.

"I could not find any wood," he said sadly as he stood watching the Baby.

"It is okay. Look over there." With her head, Miriam indicated the long, thick boards and slats that Shalev had broken off the fence and a large pile of twigs and branches.

Yosef looked at Shalev and smiled.

Shalev backed away shyly.

Without delay, Yosef began gathering the wood, small twigs, and branches the birds had gathered, and soon a small fire was blazing.

The animals looked on with moist dark eyes and basked in the soft, tender, loving moments of New Life.

Miriam was about to lay the Baby on the hay, when Shalev with all his strength pushed a small manger toward her, and looking at the Ox, she smiled and slowly rested the Baby on the hay of the manger.

"Miriam, are you cold?"

"No, Yosef, how could I be? And you?"

"How could I be?"

They both smiled at each other and for the first time since these visitors arrived, the animals felt left out of what was taking place.

"Do you need anything, Miriam?"

"I am a little weak and hungry but it will pass."

"Moo! Moo!"

"Hava, what is wrong?" Shalev asked.

"I am full. I have milk! After all these years, I feel milk. Moo! Moo!" she sounded loudly.

Yosef quickly got a bowl, walked to Hava, and softly began milking her.

"Oh, this is unbelievable! How could this be?" Hava asked as her eyes moistened with happiness.

"Cluck! Cluck!" Ova was heard saying. All the animals turned and looked at her as she shouted loudly, "Look! I have laid eggs! I have laid eggs!"

Yosef gave the bowl of milk to Miriam to hold and then he walked to Ova as she stood away from her eggs. He carefully gathered the eggs.

"Oh my, they have something to eat and grow strong with, thanks to you, Hava, and you, Ova."

"Listen!"

The stable animals listened, pitching their ears as they heard the sounds of song.

"It is the birds singing," Hava said.

"No, my friend, they sound like humans!" Ova said.

"And their singing sounds so beautiful," Hava added as she walked over and rested beside the manger.

"I do not think it is birds or humans. They sound like angels—a lot of angels," Shalev said.

Eliyah walked over to the manger and rested beside it, as his and Hava's body and breath gave the Babe some warmth.

Miriam gave the bowl of milk to Yosef and slowly lay beside the manger and rested, and soon she dozed off.

Yosef walked to her and covered her with a heavy blanket. He went to the Child in the manger and covered the Babe. He then knelt by the manger and stood watch over the Child and mother sleeping so peacefully.

Later over the fire, he heated Hava's milk in a small container and then placed Ova's eggs in the milk to boil them.

"I feel something special about this Babe," Ova said calmly.

"You know, I was feeling and thinking the same thing," Hava said.

"Yes, I agree, there is a special feeling, as though I am supposed to know who this Babe is," Shalev said, moving closely to the manger.

"Eliyah, you are strangely quiet. Do you feel what we feel?"

"Yes, from the first time I was taken by Yosef, and even more when I saw Miriam and when I carried her, I felt a special something. Then one night I heard my master and mistress speaking. I heard them speak of the Son of God being born and what this would mean to all the people and the world. Strangely, later that night as they slept, a white dove came and hovered over them all through the night. It was so amazing! Each and every night, thereafter, no matter where we stopped or when we stopped, while they slept the white dove came and hovered over them. Just the other day as we were nearing Bethlehem, I began speaking aloud about what I had seen and began to question what it all meant, when…"

"When what?" Hava asked.

"No, I cannot speak it, for you will truly think the dumb donkey is truly dumb," Eliyah said.

"Oh, come on, speak up. Look who you are speaking to—three old worn-out servants of mankind…"

"…who have received a miracle to do more for mankind," Eliyah interrupted Shalev.

The four animals looked at each other.

"Yes," Shalev said as he realized the truth in the dumb donkey's words.

I laid eggs again, Ova said to herself. *That was a wonder.*

"He's right…I had milk again," Hava said. "That had to be a miracle!" She looked at Eliyah. "Just like your limp," she concluded.

"Yes, just like my limp." Eliyah surveyed the others. "You now must know."

"Know what?" Ova said with confusion.

Eliyah wet his lip with his long tongue and said slowly, "As we approached Bethlehem and I was speaking aloud, I believe Miriam heard me and she said, 'Eliyah, you have been so good to us, and because of this you have earned the right to know that I carry the Son of God, whose name will be Jesus. You have been blessed, as will all your ancestors for the kindness you have done for the Son of God.'"

"You mean she heard you? But that is unheard of! No human ever heard us speaking. Only other animals can hear our voices," Shalev said.

"I thought you would not believe me," Eliyah said with regret.

"No, I believe you, but it is very hard to imagine. It is frightening to know this. Humans have not heard us speak for centuries."

"Unless they were angels or important people to God or…." Ova stopped and looked quickly at the others.

"God, Himself. God always heard us. He is the One who talks to us," Hava spoke as if she were reciting her thoughts.

"Now you know," Eliyah said softly as he moved closer to the manger. "God is with us."

Yosef bent down, picked up the child reverently, and held him carefully in his arms.

"Someone is coming," Shalev gave an alert.

"Yes, I hear them. It is humans," Ova said.

"It's the shepherds," Hava added. "Oh, I wish they had not decided to visit. I want more time with Miriam, Yosef, and the Babe."

Yosef faced the animals.

"Hava, you have been most kind to us. Thank you for your milk. And Ova, thank you for the eggs and you, Shalev, thank you for your strength. God, I am sure, is so pleased with you that He will bless you as He has blessed all creation with the birth of His Son. What you have done will be remembered by many, and many will know of you," Yosef said with a wide smile on his face. "But I am afraid your time is over."

"He knew our names…," Ova said.

"He spoke to us…," Shalev added.

"Because he heard us," Hava concluded.

"All in the animal kingdom was heard tonight," Yosef said as he turned and faced the slow, curious, and cautious shepherds coming up the road to the stable.

"Now let us see what mankind will do with knowing what you know, my animal friends."

◆

One Christmas Eve at our feast of *La Veglia*—the dinner of "the Seven Fishes"—I began our meal with this story. Before me that Christmas Eve, seated at a table the length of my house, was my family including my brother and brothers-in-law, my sister and sisters-in-law, my sons and daughters-in-law, all my eight grandchildren, my many nephews and nieces, my Aunt Rita, my cousin Mary Jane's family, and my wife and me—all forty-eight of us. It was a crowded room filled with some of the living of our family. Present also, assuredly, were all those who were living with the Lord.

When I finished the story, everyone sat in silence and stillness.

"So this Christmas Eve, as we enjoy this night of nights and find peace with all things created by God, let us all understand the value of family and friends as did those in that stable long ago.

"*Buon Natale. Mangi bene.*"

Merry Christmas. Eat well.

◆ THE THUMBPRINT OF GOD ◆

Nonna had the greatest respect for two of nature's delights: birds and trees. Knowing this made me love to watch her feed the birds with breadcrumbs from our family table, and to gaze upon her face as she followed the flight of a bird across the sky. I could see what I believed to be envy in her eyes when she watched a bird in flight; for birds were able to soar and glide and glimpse transcendent worlds—they could go where Nonna could not. Sometimes when we were walking along the street, or if we were in the house and Nonna was talking and she heard the chirp of a bird, she would become distracted, if only for a moment, and listen to the song of her friends.

"Birds," she often said, "are the singers of the world. Before Caruso, Como, or Sinatra, the greatest songs were already sung by the birds because they sang for God. Everyone else copied them."

She once told me that God matched birds and trees in perfect harmony because the tree was the home for the birds and the birds were the voices of the trees. They sang and filled the trees with their happy voices.

Likewise, I loved to watch her look at a tree.

If the tree was young, her countenance would reflect kindness and a hint of motherly concern, which was the same expression she turned toward her family. If it was a big tree her expression was one of awe, which was the way she looked upon a family member who had done something great in her eyes.

Trees are difficult to find when you live in a city, but we were blessed by God with a park that was only a block from our house, and Nonna would walk to this park in all kinds of weather—hot or cold, wet or dry—and at any time of the day if she needed to be refreshed. In this park was a tree that was especially beloved to Nonna, and she would take every opportunity to visit it. When we came home from church Nonna would often take the long way home just so that she could spend a few moments with her tree. With each and every visit she would stop and say to whomever she was with, "Look at the greatness of God's creation."

She even had a special name for this tree. She always called it "*Il cappuccio dorato del Dio*"—the golden hood of God; and that was because its leaves would turn a bright, golden yellow in the autumn.

During the winter months, when she walked past her special tree, she would slow down and regard its barren branches with deep sadness. It seemed to repose in quiet illness, or in death, but Nonna would speak to the tree and say, "Ah, my friend, by God's commands, you sleep."

During the spring and summer months she would walk about the tree and bask in its beauty, welcoming the new leaves; or she would linger in the cool shade of its branches.

On one particular day in early autumn, as we returned from Mass, we found ourselves standing beneath this tree at the base of its trunk. Its bright, golden-yellow leaves covered us. The great limbs, bearing hundreds of branches of every size and thousands of leaves, stretched far from us and from its trunk. From where we stood the tree looked twice as big as it ever had. The lush weight of so many leaves seemed to draw the branches close to the ground. The clustered leaves wove a canopy so thick that we could not see the blue sky between them. All that could be seen were layers and layers of buttery yellow leaves swaying to the rhythm of the breeze.

It was at that enthralling moment that I understood why Nonna had called this tree "the golden hood of God."

Nonna's eyes were transfixed. She slowly spun around and around, captured by all that was about her. Her face reflected the golden glow of the leaves. She looked like a child watching fireworks for the first time or gleefully catching the first glimpse of the lights on a Christmas tree.

Though I rejoiced to be a witness of her delight, I could not share it with her; instead, I was frightened by the enormity of the tree. The feeling of being enclosed and seemingly cut off from the rest of the city added to my fears.

"Do you feel the might of God, Vinzee?" Nonna asked, as she slowly spun around. "Do you feel the beauty of God? And the goodness of God? How could someone say there is no God when there is this sight in the world?"

She continued turning around and around.

I didn't answer her, but I followed her example and began to turn around and around as well. I wanted to feel what she was feeling, but instead I became dizzy and began to stagger.

Nonna grabbed me to prevent me from falling and getting dirty. Her face beamed.

"Come," she said, "let us walk out from under this 'golden hood of God' and see other things in life that are beautiful."

Hand in hand, we walked out from under the tree and headed home and as we walked, I continued to study her face. She seemed to be far away, lost in a mystical world. All I could see were the ordinary streets and common sights of South Philadelphia.

Before long, the tree slept throughout the winter and into spring, when it awoke and came groggily back to life.

Then one summer day when the tree was in full bloom, we had a terrible storm that lasted for hours. Immediately Nonna put our house into storm alert. The first thing she did was light a number of candles: one for each member of the family who was out of the house, whether they were working or at school. The dining table, on which small vigil candles always burned for our family members who were in the military, now flickered with greater light. As each absentee returned home, they were greeted with a cup of coffee, or tea with a small amount of *anisette*, or hot, homemade soup. After seeing to the returnee's comfort, she would then slip quietly to the dining room table and blow out one of the candles, uttering a small prayer of thanks.

During this summer storm she ordered that all electrical appliances, which she believed attracted lightening, be disconnected; and no one was permitted to sit near a window, "because lightening could strike you through it." So those of us who were home sat in the dark in the middle of the house, with the candles on the dining room table flickering and giving us light.

We could hear Nonna whispering rapidly from her place in the kitchen, and after an especially loud crack of thunder or a particularly vivid flash of lightening, we heard her cry aloud for God's protection.

Everything in the path of that storm seemed to shake and quiver. The wind ripped through the streets, tossing papers and street debris in the air. The few houses on our block that had awnings lost them to the wind.

When the storm was over, the wooden poles, which held the American flags that had flapped proudly from many homes, were broken, leaving the flags hanging soggy and wet, but still defiant. The large banner that hung in the middle of our street showing our neighborhood's participation in the Second World War was ripped and torn. Telephone and electrical wires had been ripped from their poles. Homes were blackened from power failures and many homes had flooded basements. We heard radio reports of center city department store windows being shattered, and of drivers losing control of their cars and crashing into store fronts or other cars. The trolley cars were stopped because the power plant had been hit by lightning and because the storm had flooded many streets, making it impossible for them to run.

After the storm had passed I decided to take a walk and see for myself just how bad the damage was. As I walked along, I knew that the beautiful "golden hood of God" could not have escaped unscathed; but I was not prepared for the sight which greeted me, for the tree had been damaged far more than I had anticipated. Many of its branches had snapped, and the white interior of the tree could be seen like open wounds. The many smaller branches that had cracked and fallen to the ground had been blown away by the wind, leaving empty, gaping places in what was left of its canopy. The branches of the tree that had once spread out and over the park now seemed to have collapsed inside itself. The greatness of the tree shared its destruction, for its falling limbs had done a great deal of damage to nearby homes, cars, and wooden park benches.

"The tree sounded as if it were moaning just before one of the branches snapped," I heard one neighbor say.

"It was so painful to hear. It was such a beautiful tree," said another.

Having seen all that I could bear to see, I turned away and sadly walked home.

When I arrived I told Nonna that her favorite tree had been damaged, and she instantly became very sad. I saw tears in her eyes. I stood by her, hoping that my presence would console her; but grown-ups could not be easily cheered the way children could be, and I quickly realized that my presence was of little help.

"Oh Nonna," I said lightly, with hopes of easing her sadness, "it was only a tree and there are so many other trees in the world to enjoy."

She looked at me for a long time and then took a deep breath, drawing herself to an upright position. She gave me a small smile.

"One tree is not the same as another tree, Vinzee. Trees are different just as people are different, because every tree is a special tree. Like people, each tree has a special purpose in life. The tree in the park was a sign of God's beautiful mind and it was for all of us to see, and to come to understand that beauty. Every time I saw that tree, I was filled with hope and I felt free. I am certain God knew the tree was tired and that it needed a rest. I guess it served its purpose and needed to go away to make room for another tree, but still I will miss my friend."

"Nonna?" I said in confusion; for she had been thinking aloud.

"Yes, I know. I am talking over your head. But you see, Vinzee, trees are free things in God's world. They grow wherever they can and they grow as high and as wide as they want. God dresses each tree's small branches with green leaves, which is the color of hope and life. Did you know that? Well, it is true; and each autumn, God redresses His trees with brown leaves because they have done something good for the earth, or red leaves because they have reflected his fiery sun, or yellow leaves because they are royalty among the other things in creation. In the winter, God undresses the trees and puts them to sleep, and they dream of a new spring; a new life. Each spring and summer God wakes the trees up because they have trusted and hoped in Him. So, God once again dresses the trees in green because they slept with hope during the winter."

She stopped and turned away before continuing.

"From the size of that tree, I would say it had lived a long time. It had seen a lot, and it had a long history. You know, it really is a pity that trees cannot talk to us; we would learn a lot from what they saw and knew. They probably could tell us many good stories about what they saw and witnessed. Sometimes I wish God had made it possible for all of His creation to talk to each other. What a beautiful time that would be."

She reached for a tissue and blotted her tears.

"You know the story of the Tower of Babel, Vinzee? Well, I remember hearing that before the tower was built, all the living things in the world were able to talk to each other; and because we humans wanted to be as high as God in the sky and not reach out to each other on earth, we lost the blessing of being able to talk to other things in creation. Now the animals and plants talk only to each other and we cannot hear them or their secrets or their stories. You know, they can hear us, and they know all about us because they watch us and live with us. I believe and I am sure that they are not that happy with what they see or hear from us."

She began to return to the kitchen, and I followed timidly.

"Oh well," she sighed. "God knows what He needs. After all, the tree was His."

"Nonna, I don't understand. How can something that can't think know what it is supposed to do?"

She stopped and turned to face me.

"Sometimes I forget that you are so young," she said, looking down at me and running a hand through my blond hair. "A tree, like everything created by God, has a purpose. Things like trees, rivers, and mountains serve God just by existing."

She shook her index finger in the air. She did this when she had just remembered a story or when a story was in the making, so I waited with anticipation.

"You know, I once heard a story about three small trees. Come have some coffee; I'm going to tell you about it."

I rushed into the kitchen and went directly to the metal cabinet to get the cups while Nonna got the milk and Karo, and soon we were sitting at the table together.

She leaned forward and rested her arms on the table. Her face was beaming with anticipation. My own attention was fixed upon her as she began.

"Deep in the forest many years ago, a big tree had little baby trees. These three baby trees were proudly growing near their mommy. You know, Vinzee, I'll bet that big mommy tree was as big and as old as our friend in the park—but anyway, these small trees were related to each other—like brothers and sisters. One day a man who took care of trees came into the forest and saw the small trees. He decided that he would leave one tree in the forest and take the other two baby trees with him, so he started digging. When he was finished, he carefully pulled the two small trees from the ground and wrapped their roots and put them in his truck and drove away. As he drove along the empty highway he came to a place that he thought was a good spot to plant one of the small trees. After all, there were no trees along the highway and a tree would make the road look prettier. So he stopped his truck on the side of the road and began to dig a big hole in the ground. He carefully put one of the baby trees into the hole and left. Driving many miles further he came to a spot in the city where there was a patch of earth in the midst of all the concrete. He realized that the city should have something beautiful and green also, so he stopped and dug another big hole and put the other baby tree into the ground and drove away.

"In the years that passed, the three small trees—one in the forest, one by the roadside, and one in the city—continued to grow and as they grew they watched the world move and they saw the changes that took place in the people that lived and moved around them. They saw wars, fires, and storms; loves and hatreds. They saw happiness and sadness. They saw people hurrying and resting. They saw people come and they saw people go.

"Sometimes people would stop and stay with them and appreciate them, and the trees would sway and dance happily in the wind because they knew they were great creatures that God created. They knew they had been given a purpose: to give joy to other creatures in God's world.

"Now the tree that stayed in the forest grew up to be very tall and strong. The birds and animals in the forest built houses on his branches and in his trunk. He sheltered the wolf and the fox in the rain; he even welcomed the snakes that strolled along him. He scratched the bear's back when the bear had an itch, and allowed the deer to sharpen their horns against his bark. In the summertime the spiders, bees, and butterflies played and danced upon him. But one day, the forest men came and cut him down. They sent him to a big factory where they cut him up and shaped him and used him to make furniture for people to use and enjoy.

"The second tree, who had been planted along the highway, also grew and became tall and strong. Passing cars would often stop, and people would get out and visit the tree. Some of the people would have picnics beneath her many branches. Some would stop to look at the countryside or breathe in the fresh air; others came to relax, to sit, or sleep in her cooling shade. This tree helped stop the rain from flooding the road by drinking all the rainwater that soaked the ground.

"One day during a snowstorm, a car skidded off the icy road and hit the tree. No one was hurt because the tree had stopped the car from falling into the nearby ravine and into the deep, cold river, but the tree was damaged, so she was cut down and sent to a factory. There she was chopped and sold as firewood to warm people. Some of her wood was reshaped into big long planks and used to help build a bridge across the river where she had once stood.

"The third tree, the one planted in the city, also grew up and became tall and strong. She had the loveliest purpose of all, for a school was built near her and she stood in the middle of the schoolyard. She shaded the children and was used as home base when the children played baseball or tag. Teachers would point to the tree through the classroom window and teach the children about the many different kinds of trees that God had created. Parents who took their children to school would look at the tree, and silently thank her for being so pretty for their children to enjoy and for providing shade for them. Now because trees can hear, this tree heard how much the children and the grown-ups appreciated her. She enjoyed the laughter and joy that came from the children as they played and walked around her. Because she was so happy, she grew tall and wide, so tall and wide, in fact, that she began to shade even the school building; this kept some of the classrooms cool and saved the children from the hot sun while they studied. Finally, one day, two swings were hung from her strongest branches. Now the children had a plaything in their schoolyard. As time went on, she watched many children graduate from the school and later she saw these students come back as parents with their own children. She heard their silent 'thank you' for the joy they had received from her and for the good she was now doing for their children. All this time, she silently stood guard and protected the school and the children.

"Many, many years passed, and the tree grew bigger and bigger, and older and older. Her arms ached from the swings now and the children playing around her seemed to disturb her more and more. One spring the tree didn't fully come awake; she had only a few leaves. The principal of the school had the swings taken down because the tree was tired and weak. At the end of the school year, some men came and they cut her down. They took her to a factory where she was cut up into little pieces, and paper was made from her wood. When school started again, the tree was inside the school, being used by the children as textbooks and copybooks."

Nonna stopped and slowly lifted the cup of coffee to her lips. After taking a delicate sip, she returned the cup to its saucer.

"Do you now see," she said, "why I told you that every tree has a purpose?"

I nodded. She knew that I understood, and that I now had a greater respect for trees. I could see that she was happy, and I, in turn, was happy, because I had learned something new and had another story to remember.

We continued to drink our coffee in silence.

For days after this conversation, on the way home from school, I passed the tree and looked at its broken limbs and was very unhappy. When returning from Mass, Nonna would go home by a different route, so as not to be saddened by the sight of her ravaged tree.

One day some men came and began sawing the big branches into little pieces. As I stood watching, I began to imagine that these branches were going to be used as furniture or firewood or paper and I wasn't so sad, because I innocently believed that the tree would grow back as the great big tree she was before the storm.

The next day as I came home from school, I walked by the tree and saw that the branches were gone. All that was left was the naked trunk standing alone. I went home and sadly reported to Nonna what was left of her tree.

A few weeks later the rest of the tree was cut down. My cousins and many of my friends stood beside me as we watched the men cut the trunk into big logs and little pieces of kindling. When they had finished, they took everything away and left only a big stump in the ground.

Not long after the tree was hauled away, three skinny baby trees were planted where the huge tree once stood, but the park never looked the same again.

That Sunday after Mass, Nonna and I walked to the park and looked at the stump. We were filled with reverence and sadness. Nonna let out a long sigh. I looked down and saw how many rings the stump had and realized that Nonna was right: the tree had lived a long, long life.

"Vinzee, do you remember me telling you that trees belong to God?"

"Yes, Nonna, I do." I would always remember everything she had told me about trees.

"Look at the stump. Do you know what all those rings are?"

"Yes, Nonna, they tell us how old a tree is."

"No. Look more closely, and you will see that those round marks are proof of ownership—they are the thumbprint of God."

◆ LAST COFFEE WITH NONNA ◆

Before going to bed on Sunday, May 5, 1946, I knelt down by the side of my bed and asked God to take my Nonna, for she had suffered nine long months with cancer. To see her suffer more was not how I thought God was showing mercy; besides, it became impossible to watch her suffer more. I also did this because Nonna had asked me to pray for her that night. I believed that she was certain she would be before God shortly.

Nonna died at three o'clock Monday, May 6.

My mother was with her all night and watched Nonna die. After my mother bathed Nonna, combed her hair, and arranged her legs and hands, she called the sleeping family, and it was then that the tears came.

Nonna's funeral was one of the most talked about funerals in our neighborhood. Many years before, Nonna had seen the movie *Imitation of Life* with her favorite movie star, Colette Colbert. In that film, Louise Beaver dies and her casket is carried in an ornamented carriage drawn by white horses. After seeing this movie, Nonna declared that when she died she wanted to be buried just like Louise Beaver. Most in the family took this request to heart and remembered it when she died.

Though the war was over in Europe, we were still at war in Asia. Many of Nonna's male family members were still on military duty. Thankfully, most of them had been in the European theater of the war, so the family decided to bring all of Nonna's family home for the funeral. In order to do that, we had to give the armed services time to gather them up. So Nonna was viewed in the parlor of her house for five days with plans of burying her on Saturday, the day before Mother's Day. By Saturday most of my service relatives had made it home.

Of course, we could not give her a carriage and horses; we couldn't afford it. So my mother, Aunt Jenny, Aunt Rita, and Uncle Lawrence did the next best thing, they had her casket carried from her house to King of Peace Church on the shoulders of professional pallbearers. The walk was six city blocks. Along the way, many people stood watching. Others were crying while many more just stood quietly by as their silence filled the streets with great respect. Quite a few of the people in my books about Nonna were among the watchers. I noticed as we passed, many joined in the procession to the church.

Throughout the walk, I held my head high with great pride and recalled the countless things Nonna had done for her neighbors. I was surprised by my composure, but it seemed only natural I wanted them to know that nothing really had changed, that Nonna and I were just walking the streets and passing by them. I nodded my head to acknowledge them and they all seemed to understand.

My cousin Joe and I were to serve as altar boys at her Funeral Mass. It was the most difficult thing I had to do. Till this day, I do not know how I managed to serve that Mass. To walk around Nonna's casket without talking to her, or hearing her voice, or giving her a kiss was unnatural.

When we arrived at the cemetery, every one was given a flower to put on the casket before it was lowered into the ground. For some reason, I did not get a flower. My cousin Dolly was standing beside me holding my arm so tight that I think it turned blue from lack of blood. In a last-ditch effort to be a part of my family and give my Nonna a flower, I reached down and picked up a soiled carnation and placed it on the casket just as it began to descend. It was the first and only time I gave Nonna a flower.

Many days after this ordeal, I believed that I had helped God decide to take Nonna. I was angry that I was so weak to have prayed for her to die. I also believed that my soiled flower was not worthy of Nonna and that putting the flower on her casket had caused the casket to descend. I felt alone and so confused during this time. I prayed for help and spent hours in church before and after every Mass. And I cried.

It was not easy walking past Nonna's bedroom. Thank God the family kept the door closed. It was also difficult walking into the back kitchen. When I did go to the back kitchen, I made sure someone was with me. I could not be alone in that room. There were certain dinners and meals I could not eat because they reminded me of Nonna, but mostly because they did not taste like Nonna's cooking.

Soon the emptiness had widened to walking the streets without her, going to stores without her, attending Mass without her, saying prayers without her, doing homework without her. It became overwhelming, and I mourned alone and deeply.

One day about a month after Nonna died when I was at my worst, without realizing it I walked into the back kitchen, alone. I stopped short of the archway to the kitchen. When I realized what I had done, I quickly tried to turn but couldn't. I froze, for there on the table was a cup. It was empty. It most likely had been innocently left behind, but to me, at that moment, it was something more. It was a sign just for me.

I walked slowly to the table and the cup. My mouth was dry. I was all empty and without need or want. My eyes flooded with tears and my chest felt tight as a drum. Automatically, I slowly walked to the cabinet, got two spoons, Karo, paper napkins, the milk, and finally another cup. I set the table then walked to the gas range and picked up the coffee pot. I walked back to the table and poured coffee into the cups—one last final cup—and sat opposite Nonna's place.

I longed for her voice and to hear one more story and one more answer to one more stupid question, but the room remained silent, still, and empty. I wanted to say something, for I knew she was there, but I couldn't get any words out. Besides, I was so afraid that if I did speak I would become a sobbing mess.

Unexpectedly there the smell of baking, cooking gravy, garlic, and coffee. From out of the past the back kitchen exhaled the sound of laughter, the shuffle of feet, the clamor of dishes and pots, and the cling-clang of a spoon being stirred in a coffee cup.

Nonna was around me.

Then I heard Nonna say, *"Ah, Vinzee, il caffè era buono. Che ha fatto altro abbiamo bisogno di?"* Ah, Vince, the coffee was good. What else did we need?

I raised my coffee cup to my lips, perhaps as a toast or just as a normal thing. My salty tears slipped into the coffee, changing the taste ever so slightly, yet enough to be noticed.

Sometime later, away from this life, a cup of coffee awaited me, but on that day it was my last coffee with Nonna.

About Leonine Publishers

Leonine Publishers LLC makes fine Catholic literature available to Catholics throughout the English-speaking world. Leonine Publishers offers an innovative "hybrid" approach to book publication that helps authors as well as readers. Please visit our web site at www.leoninepublishers.com to learn more about us. Browse our online bookstore to find more solid Catholic titles to uplift, challenge, and inspire.

Our patron and namesake is Pope Leo XIII, a prudent, yet uncompromising pope during the stormy years at the close of the 19th century. Please join us as we ask his intercession for our family of readers and authors.

Do you have a book inside you? Visit our web site today. Leonine Publishers accepts manuscripts from Catholic authors like you. If your book is selected for publication, you will have an active part in the production process. This book is an example of our growing selection of literature for the busy Catholic reader of the 21st century.

www.leoninepublishers.com

www.ingramcontent.com/pod-product-compliance
Lightning Source LLC
Chambersburg PA
CBHW032003040426
42448CB00006B/469